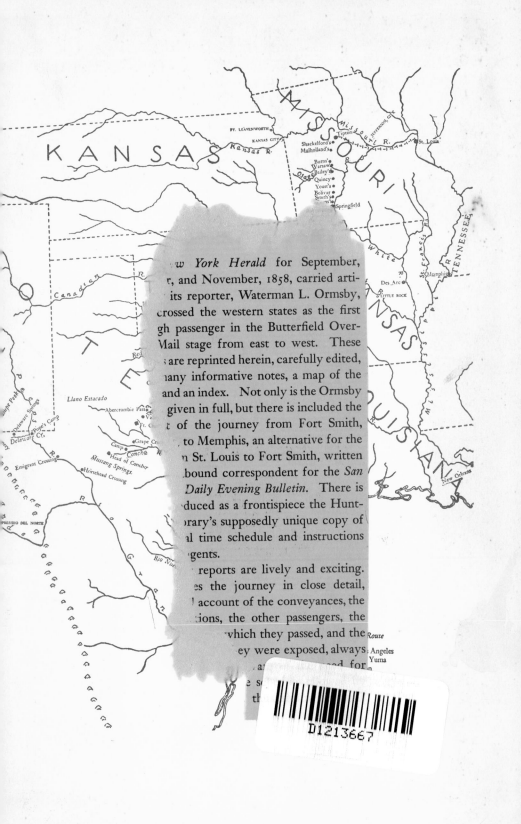

KANSAS

MISSOURI

FT. LEAVENWORTH
KANSAS CITY
Kansas R.
Shackelford's
Mulholland's
Burns
Warsaw
Bailey's
Quincy's
Youst's
Bolivar
Smith's
Springfield

Missouri R. JEFFERSON CY Tipton St. Louis

White

TENNESSEE
Memphis

Des Arc
LITTLE ROCK

Canadian R.

Red

Llano Estacado

Abercrombie Pass
Ft. C
Camp Grape Cr
Concho R.
Head of Concho
Mustang Springs
Horsehead Crossing

Emigrant Crossing

Guadalupe Peak
Delaware Springs
Pope's Camp
Delaware Cr.

Presidio del Norte

Rio Nueces

Rio Grande

w *York Herald* for September,
r, and November, 1858, carried arti-
its reporter, Waterman L. Ormsby,
crossed the western states as the first
gh passenger in the Butterfield Over-
Mail stage from east to west. These
are reprinted herein, carefully edited,
many informative notes, a map of the
and an index. Not only is the Ormsby
given in full, but there is included the
t of the journey from Fort Smith,
to Memphis, an alternative for the
n St. Louis to Fort Smith, written
bound correspondent for the *San
Daily Evening Bulletin.* There is
duced as a frontispiece the Hunt-
rary's supposedly unique copy of
al time schedule and instructions
gents.

reports are lively and exciting.
es the journey in close detail,
account of the conveyances, the
ions, the other passengers, the
which they passed, and the Route
ey were exposed, always, Angeles
a Yuma

New Orleans

LOUISIANA

ARKANSAS

St Francis

The Butterfield Overland Mail

SPECIAL INSTRUCTIONS.

In order to carry out this undertaking, it is necessary that the following Instructions be strictly observed by all Employés of the Company.

TO CONDUCTORS, AGENTS, DRIVERS & EMPLOYÉS.

1.—It is expected that all employés of the Company will be at their posts at all times, in order to guard and protect the property of the Company. Have teams harnessed in ample time, and ready to proceed without delay or confusion. Where the coaches are changed, have the teams hitched to them in time. Teams should be hitched together and led to or from the stable to the coach, so that no delay can occur by their running away. All employés will assist the Driver in watering and changing teams in all cases, to save time.

2.—When a stage is seriously detained by accident or otherwise, the Conductor or Driver will have the same noted on way bill and note book, and report fully to the Superintendent at first station the nature and cause of such delay.

3.—Conductors should never lose sight of the mails for a moment, or leave them, except in charge of the driver or some other employé of the Company, who will guard them till his return. This rule must not be deviated from under *any circumstances*. They will also report to the Superintendent in all cases if Drivers abuse or mis-manage their teams, or in any way neglect or refuse to do their duty.

4.—The time of all employés is expected to be at the disposal of the Company's Agents, in all cases, at stations where they may be laying over. Their time belongs to leave his station without personally comparing the way-bill with the passengers, and knowing that they agree. Each Station Agent will be required to note the time of arrival and departure of each stage at his station, both on the way-bill and on a book kept for that purpose, giving the Driver and Conductor's name and cause of delay, if any has occurred.

10.—Superintendents will report to the President and Treasurer of the Company, and to each other, the names of the persons authorised to receipt fare on way-bill. No others than those named by them will be allowed to receipt fare.

11.—The rates of fare will, for the present, be as follows: between the Pacific Railroad terminus and San Francisco, and between Memphis and San Francisco, either way, through tickets, $200. Local fares between Fort Smith and Fort Yuma not less than 10 cents per mile for the distance traveled. Between Fort Yuma and San Francisco, and between Fort Smith and the Railroad terminus, the rate of fare will be published by the Superintendents of those divisions.

12.—The meals and provisions for passengers are at their own expense, over and above the regular fare. The Company intend, as soon as possible, to have suitable meals at proper places prepared for passengers at a moderate cost.

COMPANY.

LE BETWEEN

FRANCISCO, CAL.

GOING EAST.

AVE.	DAYS.		Hour.	Distance, Place to Place.	Time allowed.	Av'ge Miles per Hour.
				Miles.	No.Hours	
cisco, Cal.	Every Monday & Thursday,		8.00 A.M			
's Ferry, "	"	Tuesday & Friday,	11.00 A.M	163	27	6
"	"	Wednesday & Saturday,	5.00 A.M	82	18	4½
(Via Los Angelos to)	"	Thursday & Sunday,	9.00 A.M	127	28	4½
ardino, "	"	Friday & Monday,	5.30 P.M	150	32½	4½
1a, "	"	Sunday & Wednesday,	1.30 P.M	200	44	4½
r,* Arizona	"	Monday & Thursday,	7.30 P.M	135	30	4½
"	"	Wednesday & Saturday	3.00 A.M	141	31½	4½
Farewell,	"	Thursday & Sunday,	8.00 P.M	184½	41	4½
Tex.	"	Saturday & Tuesday,	5.30 A.M	150	33½	4½
ver, (Em. Crossing.)	"	Monday & Thursday	12.45 P.M	248½	55¼	4½
lbourn, "	"	Wednesday & Saturday	1.15 A.M	165	36½	4½
knap, "	"	Thursday & Sunday,	7.30 A.M	136	30¼	4½
"	"	Friday & Monday,	4.00 P.M	146½	32½	4½
th, Ark.	"	Sunday & Wednesday,	1.00 P.M	205	45	4½
lle, Mo.	"	Monday, & Thursday,	6.15 A.M	65	17¼	3⁷⁄₉
d, "	"	Tuesday & Friday,	8.45 A.M	100	26½	3⁷⁄₉
Terminus, "	"	Wednesday & Saturday	10.30 P.M	143	37¾	3⁷⁄₉
Louis, Mo., & } mphis, Tenn. }	"	Thursday & Sunday,		160	10	16

are particularly directed to use every possible exertion to get the Stages through in quick

en without injury.
ch driver increase his speed over the average per hour enough to gain the necessary time for

each driver on the route loses fifteen (15) minutes, it would make a total loss of time, on the
loss of sixteen and one half (16½) hours, or, the best part of a day.
s.
are under heavy forfeit if the mail is behind time.
must also report the same fully to their respective Superintendents.

JOHN BUTTERFIELD.
Pres't.

No. 1]

OVERLAND MAIL

THROUGH TIME SCHEDU

ST. LOUIS, MO., MEMPHIS, TENN. } & SAN

GOING WEST.

LEAVE.		DAYS.	Hour.	Distance, Place to Place.	Time allowed.	Av'ge Miles per Hour.	L
St. Louis, Mo., & Memphis, Tenn. }		Every Monday & Thursday,	8.00 A.M	Miles.	No. Hours		San Fra
P. R. R. Terminus,	"	" Monday & Thursday,	6.00 P.M	160	10	16	Firebaug
Springfield,	"	" Wednesday & Saturday	7.45 A.M	143	$37\frac{3}{4}$	$3\frac{7}{9}$	Visalia,
Fayetteville,	"	" Thursday & Sunday,	10.15 A.M	100	$26\frac{1}{2}$	$3\frac{7}{9}$	Ft. Tejon
Fort Smith,	Ark.	" Friday & Monday,	3.30 A.M	65	$17\frac{1}{4}$	$3\frac{7}{9}$	San Ber
Sherman,	Texas	" Sunday & Wednesday,	12.30 A.M	205	45	$4\frac{1}{2}$	Fort Yu
Fort Belknap.	"	" Monday & Thursday,	9.00 A.M	$146\frac{1}{2}$	$32\frac{1}{2}$	$4\frac{1}{2}$	Gila Riv
Fort Chadbourn,	"	" Tuesday & Friday,	3.15 P.M	136	$30\frac{1}{4}$	$4\frac{1}{2}$	Tucson,
Pecos River, (Em. Crossing.)		" Thursday & Sunday,	3.45 A.M	165	$36\frac{1}{2}$	$4\frac{1}{2}$	Soldier's
El Paso,		" Saturday & Tuesday,	11.00 A.M	$248\frac{1}{2}$	$55\frac{1}{4}$	$4\frac{1}{2}$	El Paso,
Soldier's Farewell		" Sunday & Wednesday,	8.30 P.M	150	$33\frac{1}{2}$	$4\frac{1}{2}$	Pecos Ri
Tucson,	Arizona	" Tuesday & Friday,	1.30 P.M	$184\frac{1}{2}$	41	$4\frac{1}{2}$	Fort Cha
Gila River,*	"	" Wednesday & Saturday	9.00 P.M	141	$31\frac{1}{2}$	$4\frac{1}{2}$	Fort Bel
Fort Yuma,	Cal.	" Friday & Monday,	3.00 A.M	135	30	$4\frac{1}{2}$	Sherman
San Bernardino	"	" Saturday & Tuesday,	11.00 P.M	200	44	$4\frac{1}{2}$	Fort Sm
Ft. Tejon, (Via Los Angelos.)		" Monday & Thursday,	7.30 A.M	150	$32\frac{1}{2}$	$4\frac{1}{2}$	Fayettev
Visalia,	"	" Tuesday & Friday,	11.30 A.M	127	28	$4\frac{1}{2}$	Springfie
Firebaugh's Ferry,	"	" Wednesday & Saturday	5.30 A.M	82	18	$4\frac{1}{2}$	P. R. R.
(Arrive) San Francisco,		" Thursday & Sunday,	8.30 A.M	163	27	6	(Arrive) St M

This Schedule may not be exact—Superintendents, Agents, Station-men, Conductors, Drivers and all employees time, even though they may be ahead of this time.

If they are behind this time, it will be necessary to urge the animals on to the highest speed that they can be dri

Remember that no allowance is made in the time for ferries, changing teams, &c. It is therefore necessary that e meals, changing teams, crossing ferries, &c.

Every person in the Company's employ will always bear in mind that each minute of time is of importance. I entire route, of twenty-five (25) hours, or, more than one day. If each one loses ten (10) minutes it would make a total

On the contrary, if each driver gains that amount of time, it leaves a margin of time against accidents and extra delay

All hands will see the great necessity of promptness and dispatch: every minute of time is valuable as the Company

Conductors must note the hour and date of departure from Stations, the causes of delay, if any, and all particulars. The

* The Station referred to on Gila River, is 40 miles west of Maricopa Wells.

ways ready for duty.

5.—None but the Company's Superintendents or Agents who have written permission, are authorized to make or contract debts, give notes, due bills, or any obligations on account of the Company.

6.—Conductors and Drivers will be very particular, and not allow the Company's property to be abused, or neglect to report to the proper parties the repairs required.

7.—You will be particular to see that the mails are protected from the wet, and kept safe from injury of every kind while in your possession, in your division, and you will be held personally responsible for the safe delivery at the end of your route, or point of destination, of all mails and other property in your charge.

8.—The Company will not at present transport any *through* extra baggage, freights, or parcels of any description. All employés are cautioned against receiving such matter in any shape or manner, except such local business of this nature, from place to place, as will be done according to the instructions and prices to be given by the different Superintendents. You will not fail to see that all parcels, boxes or bundles carried on the stage, shall be entered on the way bill, with amount of freight to be charged, and you will be held responsible for the safe delivery, at point of destination, of all such packages. The Agent will see that the charges are paid, and articles receipted for at time of delivery. No money, jewelry, bank notes, or valuables of any nature, will be allowed to be carried under any circumstances whatever.

9.—All Superintendents, Agents, Conductors and Drivers will see particularly that every passenger shall have their names entered on the way-bill at point of departure; that their fare shall be paid in advance, and the amount entered on way-bill as paid to point of destination. No Conductor or Agent must allow any stage

M. L. KENYON, *San Francisco, Cal.*
HUGH CROCKER, *Fort Smith, Ark.*
JAMES GLOVER, *El Paso, Texas*
WM. BUCKLEY, *Fort Yuma, Cal.*
GILES HAWLEY, *Tucson, Arizona*
HENRY BATES, *Fort Belknap, Texas,*
} *Superintendents.*

ceeding 40 lbs. in any case.

14.—Passengers stopping from one stage to another, can only do so at their own risk as to the Company being able to carry them on a following stage. In cases of this nature, the Conductor or Agent at the place where they leave the stage, will endorse on the way-bill opposite their name, "Stopped over at ———." And on the way-bill of the stage in which the passenger continues his journey, the entry of his name will be made with the remark, "Stopped over from stage of the ——— (giving the date). Fare paid to ——— on way-bill of ——— (date) from ——— (name the place.)"

15.—All employés are expected to show proper respect to and treat passengers and the public with civility, as well as to use every exertion for the comfort and convenience of passengers.

16.—Agents, Conductors, Drivers and all employés will follow strictly all instructions that may be received from time to time from the Superintendents of their respective divisions.

17.—Any transactions of a disreputable nature will be sufficient cause for the discharge of any person from the employ of the Company.

18.—INDIANS. A good look-out should be kept for Indians. No intercourse should be had with them, but let them alone; by no means annoy or wrong them. At all times an efficient guard should be kept, and such guard should always be *ready* for any emergency.

19.—It is expected of every employé that he will further the interests of the Company by every means in his power, more especially by living on good terms with all his fellow-employés, by avoiding quarrels and disagreements of every kind and nature with all parties, and by the strictest attention of each and every one to his duties.

JOHN BUTTERFIELD,
President.

The
BUTTERFIELD
OVERLAND MAIL

By
WATERMAN L. ORMSBY
*Only Through Passenger on
the First Westbound Stage*

Edited By
LYLE H. WRIGHT AND JOSEPHINE M. BYNUM

THE HUNTINGTON LIBRARY
San Marino, California
1960

Contents

Introduction

CONTEMPORARY accounts of travel on the Overland
Mail Company's stage line during the years 1858 to
1861, when it was operating between St. Louis and
Memphis, the two eastern terminals, and San Francisco, are
all too few. The best narrative consists of a series of eight
articles by Waterman L. Ormsby, published in six numbers
of the *New York Herald* at intervals from September 26
to November 19, 1858. Ormsby, a special correspondent
of the *Herald*, was the only through passenger on the first
westbound stage. His articles, here reprinted,[1] supply a
graphic picture of the country through which he passed
from St. Louis to San Francisco. They furnish a full and
accurate account of the controversy that raged over the
various proposed transcontinental routes for a mail-and-
passenger stage line, which had been authorized by an act
of Congress in March, 1857. They also give the Postmaster-General's reasons for selecting the "thirty-second
parallel route," with an eastern bifurcation, and awarding
the contract to John Butterfield and his associates.

Ormsby says in his first article that, "in view of the importance of this enterprise at this time, and the bearing
which it has upon the future destinies of this country, I
propose to give you a condensed account of the origin
and history of the contract and the claims of the competing routes." From the information presented concerning

[1] The first article, which relates almost entirely to events preceding
Ormsby's trip, is placed at the end of his narrative. His second article,
published also in the September 26 issue of the *New York Herald*, begins
the record of his overland journey. The text of the account was included
in W. B. Lang's *The First Overland Mail, Butterfield Trail* (Washington,
1940).

vii

the different routes, it is evident that, before his departure from New York, he had made an exhaustive study of the overland project.[2] The fact that he traveled a considerable distance on the stage with John Butterfield, president of the Overland Mail Company, lends authority to his statements about the company. The articles covering the trip, written for the most part en route, furnish a narrative of stagecoach travel as told by an acute observer, who appreciated the dangers of such a journey without dramatizing them. The series as a whole makes an important contribution to the annals of transportation in the United States.

The mail route adopted by the Postmaster-General had two eastern terminals on the Mississippi River, one at St. Louis and the other at Memphis, the two forks converging at Fort Smith, Arkansas. From Fort Smith, the line ran through Indian Territory to Colbert's Ferry on the Texas border, thence bore to the west, over the plains of Texas, to Franklin, opposite El Paso, Mexico, crossing the dreaded Llano Estacado en route. Leaving Franklin, the road traversed the arid lands of New Mexico Territory, and entered California near Fort Yuma, on the Colorado River. At this point it dipped southward into Mexico for a short distance and re-entered California in the neighborhood of the New River, crossed the mountains (by way of Warner's ranch) to Los Angeles, and proceeded north through the San Joaquin Valley and Pacheco Pass to San Francisco, the western terminal. The route was over 2,700 miles long, and the first run of the Butterfield stages, carrying the mail and Ormsby, was made in 23 days, 23 hours.

[2] Ormsby left New York for St. Louis on Sept. 10, according to the *Los Angeles Star*, Oct. 9, 1858.

Waterman Lily Ormsby, Jr., the *Herald* correspondent, was born in New York City, December 8, 1834. His father was a prominent engraver, the author of several pamphlets on the engraving of banknotes, and one of the founders of the Continental Bank Note Company.[3] Little is known of the son's early schooling, or when he began newspaper work. During his career as a reporter he was associated with four New York newspapers, the *Herald*, *Times*, *World*, and *Sun*.

When Ormsby made the overland trip, he was twenty-three years old, a married man, and the father of a nine-months-old boy,[4] who is referred to in the articles. Ormsby did not regard his assignment entirely in the nature of a youthful adventure, but appreciated the fact that he was participating in a historical event. Upon his arrival in San Francisco, his enthusiasm for the overland mail route, and its potential place in the development of the rich and interesting country through which he had passed, was undiminished. And, even though the journey had been fatiguing, he said he was willing to repeat it. However, Mr. Harlow has stated that Ormsby returned to New York by steamer.[5]

Little or nothing has been found concerning Ormsby's activities during the next twelve years. About 1870 he

[3] For further information concerning the father, see *Dictionary of American Biography*, XIV, 55.

[4] He was born Dec. 15, 1857, and named Waterman Lily Ormsby III. His career was similar to his father's. Following graduation from the College of the City of New York, in 1876, he was a newspaper reporter, private secretary, and amanuensis, and, in 1882, was appointed secretary to the senate of the state of Pennsylvania. Two years later he became official stenographer to the supreme court in Kings County, New York—a position he retained until his death, Apr. 11, 1914. He was twice married and the father of one son and two daughters.

[5] See A. F. Harlow, *Old Waybills* (New York, 1934), p. 206.

became affiliated with the Continental Bank Note Company, holding a responsible position with that firm for fourteen years. In 1885 he was appointed official stenographer of the magistrates' court of New York City—a position in which he continued until his death on April 29, 1908.[6] He was survived by his wife, one daughter, and two of three sons, both of whom were stenographers in the New York supreme court. Ormsby always took pride in having been for many years the *de facto* president of the New York Liberal Club while Horace Greeley was nominally its presiding officer.

In the San Francisco *Daily Evening Bulletin* "Supplement" dated December 16, 1858, under the heading "Letter from Washington, Nov. 19, 1858," there occurs the charge that Ormsby was employed by the Butterfield Overland Mail Company. The item reads as follows:

The N. Y. "Herald's" Puffing Reporter of
the Butterfield Overland Route

The comments of the *Bulletin* upon the invidious attempt of parties in San Francisco to make a little capital for the New York *Herald*, by puffing its *marvelous* enterprise in dispatching a special correspondent to San Francisco *via* the Butterfield Overland Mail[7] met a cordial response here, where it is known that said

  [6] Obituary notices are to be found in the following New York newspapers for Apr. 30, 1908: *Herald, Times, World,* and *Sun.*

  [7] This refers to the editorial in the San Francisco *Daily Evening Bulletin* [hereinafter cited as *Bulletin*], Oct. 12, 1858, which reads: "Last night the real objects of the meeting [the mass meeting held to celebrate the arrival of the first overland mail] were nearly overshadowed and lost sight of, because of the attempts of one or two contemptible characters to get themselves puffed in a New York journal, by playing toady to its special reporter, who happened to be present. For the sake of quietness, we hope the effort will have succeeded and to assist it, we request said special reporter to indite a most windy and beslabering 'puff' of the mover of the resolutions complimenting the New York *Herald*."

correspondent was specially employed *at the expense of the company*, to go over the route and write it up! The mail company doubtless deserves credit for its enterprise in that respect, and it certainly had a perfect right to resort to any and every honorable measure to advertise its route and bring it into public notice; but it was an unworthy trick to try to make capital out of these facts for the *Herald*. Desperately as it needs such adventitious "boosting" nowadays, it could hardly expect the effort to pass unchallenged.

Butterfield may have furnished the *Herald* with a pass for its reporter, and may also have extended the same offer to other large newspapers; but Ormsby's account does not seem to indicate that he was employed by the overland company.

John Butterfield, president of the company, was born at Berne, New York, November 18, 1801. He had little formal education, and at an early age became a stage driver. His rise was rapid and he was soon in control of several stage lines in the state of New York. He was one of the founders of the American Express Company, which was formed in 1850.[8]

On September 16, 1857, Butterfield and his associates signed a six-year contract, at $600,000 per annum, for a semiweekly mail service between St. Louis and San Francisco. By the terms of section thirteen of the post-office appropriation bill of March 3, 1857, the company had to commence service within one year of signing. Butterfield's opponents said he could never establish a line of stations across the country and properly equip them with stock and coaches; or, if he did, the line—the longest in the world—would be too unwieldy and was thus doomed to failure.

[8] For further information about Butterfield see *Dict. Am. Biog.*, III, 374-75.

But years of staging experience, coupled with his planning and organizing ability, enabled Butterfield to make the enterprise an outstanding success. Reliable service over the route was maintained during the company's two and one-half years of operation—it was abandoned following the outbreak of the Civil War.

Several books and monographs have been published that deal more or less extensively with the Butterfield enterprise, and a short check list of titles relating to the subject has been compiled.[9] The question of the date of departure of the first mail from St. Louis and from San Francisco has caused a number of writers considerable trouble. The majority record September 15, 1858, as the date of simultaneous departure; a few set the date as September 16; and others give only the date of departure from San Francisco. This confusion is unquestionably due, at least in part, to the newspaper announcements in San Francisco and St. Louis, which stated that the first mail would leave their respective cities at the same time. Even Ormsby assumed that the western mail left on the same day as the eastern, and he did not learn differently until his stage met the eastbound one at the entrance of Guadalupe Canyon on September 28.

Actually, the stage carrying the mail for the East left San Francisco September 15, and the westbound mail left St. Louis September 16.[10] These two dates have been no-

---

[9] See William Tallack, *The California Overland Express . . . With an Introduction by Carl I. Wheat and a Check List . . . by J. Gregg Layne* ("Special Publication No. 1" of the Historical Society of Southern California; Los Angeles, 1935). The check list follows the reprint of the account that an Englishman, Tallack, gave of his ride over the Butterfield route in 1860.

[10] "The through mail to Memphis and St. Louis starts from this city at one o'clock tomorrow morning, and it is calculated by the contractors, will

ticed by a few writers, and Monas N. Squires deals with the subject rather fully.[11]

Shortly after Ormsby arrived in San Francisco two of that city's newspapers, the *Alta California* and the *Bulletin*, sent special correspondents eastward on the overland route. The *Alta*'s reporter, J. M. Farwell, covered the same ground as Ormsby, but the unidentified *Bulletin* reporter traveled from San Francisco to Memphis. The latter's article, dated "Memphis, December 8, 1858," describing the portion of his journey from Fort Smith to Memphis, is reprinted in the Appendix.

The frontispiece to the present volume is a reproduction of the first time schedule issued by the Overland Mail Company. The original was recently found in the miscellaneous papers of the Lieber collection in the Huntington Library.[12] The schedule is very rare, if not unique; no copy is recorded in Camp's revision of Wagner,[13] nor is any reference made to it in the many publications relating to the company. Ormsby, in his first article in the *Herald*, writes, "although you have already published the time table of the company, I think it will be interesting to your readers to repeat it here"; but he supplies only that part

get through inside of twenty-five days." (San Francisco *Bulletin*, Sept. 14, 1858.) "The first overland mail for San Francisco . . . takes its departure this morning from the St. Louis post office, at 7 o'clock . . . At the same time, a mail will start for the East from San Francisco." (*Ibid.*, Oct. 11, 1858, quoting from the St. Louis *Republican*, Sept. 16.)

[11] See M. N. Squires, "The Butterfield Overland Mail in Missouri," *The Missouri Historical Review*, XXVI, 331-41.

[12] The Francis Lieber papers were purchased in 1927. A survey, by C. B. Robson, of the collection, other than the miscellaneous material, is available in *The Huntington Library Bulletin*, No. 3 (Feb., 1933), pp. 135-55.

[13] H. R. Wagner, *The Plains and the Rockies . . . Revised and Extended by Charles L. Camp* (San Francisco, 1937).

of the table under the heading "Going West," or, as Ormsby designates it, "Going to San Francisco."[14] Both the *Bulletin* and the *Alta California* give the timetable, at least in part, and probably it could be found in other newspapers.[15]

The original schedule, a single sheet, measures 8½ by 14⅛ inches. An east-and-west timetable and a few company rules are printed on the recto, and a double column of "special instructions" appears on the verso. Number eleven of the instructions states that the through fare, either way, will be $200. However, the initial west-east fare was $100; the amount was increased to $200 in January, and reduced to $150 in May.[16] There is no place of printing or printer's name recorded. Possibly Heiller & Company, of New York, printed the schedule, as their name occurs on the second one, which was issued about five months later, in January, 1859. The second schedule is more elaborate, judging from two different descriptions of the only known copy.[17]

Footnotes to the text have been added only when clarification seemed necessary, or there was new or little-known information to present. The editors appreciate the fact

[14] Ormsby, when mentioning the previous publication of the timetable, refers to the *New York Herald* for Sept. 7, which prints both columns— "Going West" and "Going East."

[15] The *Bulletin* for Oct. 11 published only the timetable of the westbound stages, and reported that the eastbound stage table could not be printed, as it did not at present agree with the actual departures. The *Weekly Alta California* for Oct. 23 reprinted, with a few compositor's errors, the complete timetable as published in the *New York Herald*, Sept. 7.

[16] See San Francisco *Bulletin*, Oct. 11, 1858; Jan. 10, May 23, 1859.

[17] Wagner, *op. cit.*, item 319; Hist. Soc. of Sou. Calif. *Quarterly*, XVIII, No. 2. In addition to the description, the *Quarterly* reproduces, in facsimile, the map and four pages of the second schedule.

that some of the footnotes, particularly those relating to California, could have been expanded; however, such additional information is readily available. A number of persons mentioned in the text do not have identifying footnotes, because too slight information about them, or none at all, was found. Capitalization and punctuation have been modernized in the reprint, and obvious compositor's errors have been corrected, for the most part, without notice, but misspellings of proper names have been retained, with corrections immediately following in square brackets.

The editors wish to thank the following for their generous assistance in assembling biographical information about Ormsby: Mr. Joseph Gavit, Associate Librarian of New York State Library; Mr. Matthew Redding, of the Reference Department of the New York World-Telegram; Mr. D. G. Rogers, Director of Reference of the New York Herald-Tribune; and Mr. Donald A. Roberts, Secretary of the Associate Alumni of the College of the City of New York. Thanks are also due to Miss Alice Lerch, of the Library of Congress, for her kind help.

New York Herald, Sunday, September 26, 1858

Overland to San Francisco

On the Way to San Francisco Overland
Sept. 16, 1858

Details of the Starting of the First Mail. What the Western People Think of It. The Direction for the Mail Bag. The Route on the Pacific Railroad. Necessity of Military Protection over the Plains. A Suggestion for the Occasion, &c., &c.

I SENT you a letter, this morning, with an account of the great overland mail enterprise; but, owing to the fact that I started along with the first mail bag, I could not give you the details of the start, though I informed you that we were on the way. Although some of the St. Louis papers noticed that this important enterprise was to be commenced today, but little attention appeared to be paid it, except by the personal friends of the contractors and a few others. Indeed, I have been somewhat surprised to find that in the West—which, above all other sections

1

of the country, is to be benefitted—so little attention is paid to the great overland mail.

I could not but be impressed with the fact that your representative, then over a thousand miles from home, was the only member of the press who witnessed the deposit of the first mail bag, en route for San Francisco overland, in the cars of the Pacific Railroad Company, at St. Louis. The operation in itself was simple enough; but, as the honest Irishman passed the two diminutive bags to Mr. John Butterfield, the president of the Overland Mail Company, I could not but think that the time was not far distant when the overland mail from St. Louis would be of less insignificant proportions, and when I might look back upon that day as our fathers do now upon the time when a journey from New York to Albany was a great undertaking, and when to imagine a railroad would have been a carte blanche for the lunatic asylum. I looked forward in my imagination to the time when, instead of a wagon road to the Pacific, we should have a railroad; and when, instead of having to wait over forty days for an answer from San Francisco, a delay of as many minutes will be looked upon as a gross imposition, and of as many seconds as "doing from fair to middling."

In this view I could not allow the bags to pass me without copying the direction, just as a matter of history. Here it is, as it was branded on a stick tied to the bag:

> San Francisco, California
> Per Overland Mail
> St. Louis, Sept. 16, 1858
> Return Label by Express

There were only two small bags, as the postmaster at St.

Louis only put in such as were marked "Per Overland Mail." This was deemed advisable, so that in case of accident to the wagons the mail can be thrown across a mule, and proceed on its destination. The company have, however, taken some papers and packages for stations along the route, which they intend to deliver promptly, and, if expectations are fulfilled, to furnish the latest news up to the time of starting, in advance of the steamer that leaves on the 20th from New York.

Mr. Butterfield intended to have taken the bags from the post office at St. Louis himself, but the postmaster sent them to the railroad depot in the mail wagon, and Mr. Butterfield took charge of them there. He will accompany them as far as Springfield, Mo.[18] The mail from Memphis, which is to meet this at Fort Smith and proceed with it to San Francisco, was to have started this morning. Should it, from any unforeseen cause, be detained, I understand the Postmaster General has given instructions to wait for it, if necessary, at least a day. But you may depend upon it that Mr. Crocker, who has that part of the line under his charge, will make every effort to be up to time, and nothing but accidents which would stop any route will prevent his appearance with the Memphis mail at Fort Smith when we get there.

It should not be a matter of surprise though there should be some delays in the first journey over a comparatively new route; but, as from today the trips will become [semi-] weekly, it will doubtless not be long before the line is in good running order. As the service is to commence on the Pacific side at the same date, we shall have, if the contract is fulfilled, a semi-weekly mail arriving in San Francisco,

18 Butterfield went through to Fort Smith, as Ormsby later notes.

Memphis, and St. Louis, and completely eclipsing the news of the steamers. To insure this success, the administration of Mr. Buchanan has done much in giving to experienced men this the greatest mail contract for land service ever given.

But it must not be supposed that the wagons of this company, containing, as they will, valuable mails and packages, are to be exempt either from the designs of lawless Indians or white men. The tempting bait of an inadequately protected prize—such a prize as the overland mail will probably be after a few trips—cannot, undoubtedly, be withstood by the lawless men on the route, and the strong arm of military protection can alone be its defence. I do not mean to be understood as saying or insinuating that these mails will not go through safe, for the route includes a number of military posts, and the company has provided, from its ample means, armed protection at the weaker points. But assurance should be made doubly sure in this great national work, and the safety of the mails insured beyond peradventure.

Let any of your readers take a map of Texas and note the large number of forts which dot its western section.[19] Now, why could not the men who are here stationed be placed along the overland route, forming a chain of military posts along its line, and serving to keep the Indians north of it, where they belong? This would make effectual the large army drafts now employed in Texas,[20] and would

[19] Seventeen military posts in Texas are listed in *The Texas Almanac, for 1859* [Galveston, 1858], p. 92. For a description of the forts see Arrie Barrett, "Western Frontier Forts of Texas, 1845-1861," in West Texas Historical Association *Year Book*, VII (June, 1931), 115-39.

[20] Ormsby is referring to the large number of troops stationed throughout Texas to protect the growing settlements from hostile Indians. Many

look more like using them to some purpose. To use these men where they are now, is like scattering an army to receive the attacks of an insidious enemy. A line of military defences along this route would not only protect the mail but the country south of it, and render available all that most desirable part of Texas south of the thirty-second parallel, as well as the rich mines and fruitful lands of the Gadsen [Gadsden] Purchase in New Mexico, whose inhabitants have been so long harassed by the incursions of the Indians desolating their country. The protection would be but a fair carrying out of the stipulations under which the purchase was made. It would rapidly pave the way for rich and populous states, and render a pecuniary return far above its cost.

But I have allowed my reflections to carry me further than my facts, and have not yet told you how far the overland mail has progressed. We are now on the Pacific Railroad. But what's in a name? It is a single track road, and only extends about a hundred and sixty miles west of St. Louis. It has nearly a due west course, following the course of the Missouri to Jefferson City, the capital of the state. It has been six or seven years in the course of construction to this point, having, in the time when the river is full, hard competition with the steamboats. About thirty-seven miles from St. Louis, at Franklin (which is still an embryo town), the southwest branch, which was intended for the great Pacific road, is commenced. The idea of the

---

army posts were established, following the Mexican War, along the new frontier, and were increased as necessity demanded. See O. L. Spaulding, *The United States Army in War and Peace* (New York, 1937), pp. 227-42; A. B. Bender, "Military Posts in the Southwest, 1848-1860," *New Mexico Historical Review*, XVI, 125-47.

road at its commencement was to make it carry out its name, and in so far as it carrys the overland mail it has done so.

About eighty-eight miles from St. Louis is the Gasconade bridge, which about two years since broke down, and quite a number of prominent citizens were killed.[21] There are four tunnels on the road—in all, about three-quarters of a mile long. The rock appears to be of a soft clay nature, very flaky, and is, I believe, sometimes called cottonwood rock. The route is generally more hilly and rocky than any part of the country I have noticed, often passing the Hudson River Railroad.

There are, however, along the line large agricultural districts, and I noticed much corn, tobacco, and Chinese sugar cane growing. The latter is much grown here, though I believe it is not yet worked to obtain sugar. The syrup is said to be very excellent. This road runs through the most agricultural district of Missouri, east of Jefferson City, and strangely contrasts with the fertile prairies of Indiana and Illinois, whose vast fields of waving corn and grain can only be accounted for by the rapid introduction of agricultural labor saving machinery, which has yet to come into use here. As we rode along I saw two or three of those ungainly looking western steamboats, which on the North River would be mistaken for mud scows. One of them was aground—a situation particularly suggestive of the great difficulty with which the Big Muddy is navigated, notwithstanding the wide flat bottoms of the boats.

[21] The Gasconade bridge disaster referred to occurred Nov. 1, 1855. For details of the accident see Dorothy Jennings, "The Pacific Railroad Company," in Missouri Historical Society *Collections*, VI, No. 3 (1931), pp. 305-7.

At Jefferson City the passengers take the boats for Kansas and Leavenworth, as the road is not yet completed as far as that.[22] An extension has, however, been completed to Tipton,[23] about thirty-eight miles from Jefferson City, the road leaving the Missouri about four miles above that point and taking a more southerly course. It has been put in the hands of the company but a few months, and the road is so bad that the journey of the thirty-eight miles occupies about three hours sometimes. Beyond Jefferson City the land appears more level, with better opportunities for cultivation. As contemplated the road is to pass through Cooper, Peters, Johnson, and Jackson counties to the mouth of the Kansas River. It is, I believe, all under contract. The railroad company have a grant of a million acres of the best iron and lead region of Missouri, to assist in the construction of the southwest branch of their road.

I had but a glance at Jefferson City, as we stopped there but a few minutes; but the capitol can plainly be seen from the cars going either way, as it is on a steep eminence overlooking the river, and round which the track winds. It is built of light magnesia limestone, and though of somewhat diminutive proportions has quite a commanding appearance. The city, I believe, has about 3,000 inhabitants, but it is not visible to advantage from the railroad station.

At Tipton, Moniteau County, Mo., the end of the Pacific Railroad, the bags are first placed on the coaches of the Overland Mail Company. We left St. Louis this morn-

22 The Pacific Railroad between St. Louis and Kansas City, Mo., was completed in 1865, and extended to Leavenworth in 1866. For accounts of the railroad see R. E. Riegel, "The Missouri Pacific Railroad to 1879," *Mo. Hist. Rev.*, XVIII, 3-26; P. W. Gates, "The Railroads of Missouri, 1850-1870," *ibid.*, XXVI, 126-41; Jennings, *op. cit.*, pp. 288-314.

23 Completed the preceding July. See Jennings, p. 308.

ing at eight o'clock, and are to leave Tipton at six P.M. Thus far we are up to time. I shall mail you this at Tipton, and after that will write as the journey will permit. If I can write in the wagons with not less convenience than I have written this in the cars, you will hear from me regularly.

Overland to San Francisco

Special Correspondence of the New York Herald
In an Overland Mail Wagon,
Near Red River, Indian Territory, Sept. 20, 1858

Progress of the First Mail. Four-in-hand across the Continent. Thirty-five Hours Ahead to the Texas Border. The Route— What Is to Be Seen—How the Western People Received the Overland Mail, &c., &c., &c.

MY LAST letter was written on the Pacific Railroad, near the western terminus, and left us in anticipation of meeting the first overland mail stage at Tipton, about one hundred and sixty miles from St. Louis, which city, it will be recollected, the great overland mail left at 8 o'clock on the morning of the 16th inst. Since that time we have traveled day and night, across hills, mountains, and plains, as fast as four horses with constant relays could carry us. The teams have all been promptly ready to change, and I think that the facility of our progress has been even greater than the best hopes of the company anticipated. We are now nearly six hundred and seventy miles from St. Louis, or about one quarter of the distance of our journey.

Our general course has been west over the Pacific to a terminus, and southwest through Missouri, to Fort Smith on the Arkansas line, thence to the Red River, the border of Texas, crossing it a few miles below Preston. At Fort Smith we arrived just twenty-four hours in advance of

9

the time allotted us in the time table which you have published, which made us due at 3:30 A.M. on Monday, while
we had arrived and started before that time on Sunday.
Much to our astonishment we found that the Memphis
mail had beaten us fifteen minutes, though this was accounted for by the assertion that the Memphis postmaster
had given up the mails before time. I was thus deprived
of my anticipated privilege of writing you from Fort
Smith, and, as since then the stages have gained nine hours
more, you may readily believe I have had no opportunity
to write.

To gain thirty-two hours, as we have, on the already
close time table of the Overland Mail Company has not
given us much time to go easy over the stones. I have
given up several attempts to write, out of sheer despair,
and perhaps your printers will wish I had given up this.
Writing on Captain Rynder's[24] back in the midst of a
Tammany Hall row is not a circumstance to it. The only
sleep I have had since last Thursday morning has been
snatched in the wagons, on roads which out-Connecticut
Connecticut. Yet the new scenes which constantly meet
the view, the variegated aspect of the country, the curious
characters to be met, and the novelty of roughing it overland, are, I think, quite a recompense for any slight incon-
venience which may be experienced. But, to the details
of our journey.

The Pacific Railroad train, carrying the first overland
mail, arrived at Tipton, the western terminus of the road,

[24] Isaiah Rynders, who was head of the Empire Club, was also called
"captain" in Rynders' Grenadiers. Both of these organizations were of a
political nature, with unsavory reputations. See D. T. Lynch, *Boss Tweed*
(New York, 1927), *passim.*

situated in Moniteau County, Mo., at precisely one minute after six o'clock P.M. of Thursday, the 16th inst., being several minutes behind time. We there found the first coach ready, the six horses all harnessed and hitched, and Mr. John Butterfield, Jr., impatient to be off.

The town contains but a few hundred inhabitants, and all these seemed to have turned out for the occasion, though they made no demonstration on account of it. The place is, however, but a few months old, having been built since the completion of this end of the line, and doubtless excitements are too rare to be appreciated. They looked on with astonishment as the baggage and packages were being rapidly transferred from the cars to the coach. The latter was entirely new and had not yet held a load of passengers. It very much resembled those heavy coaches which are used in New York to convey passengers between the steamboats, car depots, and the hotels, and appeared to be quite as expensively built. In large letters over the side was the following:

> OVERLAND MAIL COMPANY

The time occupied in shifting the baggage and passengers was just nine minutes, at which time the cry of "all aboard," and the merry crack of young John Butterfield's whip, denoted that we were off. I took a note of the "following distinguished persons present," as worthy of a place in history: Mr. John Butterfield, president of the Overland Mail Company; John Butterfield, Jr., on the box; Judge Wheeler,[25] lady, and two children, of Fort

25 Ormsby refers to "Judge Wheeler," on p. 24, as the founder of two

Smith; Mr. T. R. Corbin, of Washington; and the correspondent of the *Herald*. It had been decided to take no passengers but the last named gentleman, on the first trip, but Mr. Butterfield made an exception in favor of Judge Wheeler, agreeing to take him to Fort Smith, where he intended to go himself. You will perceive, therefore, that your correspondent was the only through passenger who started in the first overland coach for San Francisco, as all the rest of the party dropped off by the time we reached Fort Smith. Not a cheer was raised as the coach drove off, the only adieu being, "Good bye, John," addressed to John, Jr., by one of the crowd. Had they have been wild Indians they could not have exhibited less emotion.

Our road for the first few miles was very fair, coursing through several small prairies, where for the first time I noticed those travelling hotels so commonly seen in the western country. These are large covered wagons, in which the owner and his family, sometimes numbering as high as a dozen, emigrate from place to place, travelling in the daytime, and camping near wood, water, and grass at night. All along the wildest western roads these hotels may be met in every direction, enlivening the way by their camp fires at night, and presenting pictures of domestic felicity which might well be emulated in certain quarters more comfortable and less homely. We rode along

---

newspapers at Fort Smith. John F. Wheeler (d. 1880), onetime printer of the *Cherokee Phoenix*, first published the Fort Smith *Herald* in June, 1847, and the *Times* in Jan., 1858. Accounts of Wheeler do not mention that he was ever a judge; apparently the title was merely by courtesy. See *Centennial History of Arkansas*, ed. D. T. Herndon (3 vols.; Chicago, 1922), I, 586; R. S. Walker, *Torchlights to the Cherokees* (New York, 1931), pp. 55-56; Althea Bass, *Cherokee Messenger* (Norman, Okla., 1936), *passim*.

at a somewhat rapid pace, because John, Jr., was determined that the overland mail should go through his section
on time; and, though his father kept calling out, "Be care-
ful, John," he assured him that it was "all right," and
drove on.

The first stopping place was at "Shackleford's," about
seven miles distant, and we seemed hardly to have become
comfortably seated in the coach before our attention was
attracted to the illumination of our destination—a recog-
nition of the occasion which seemed quite cheering after
the apparent previous neglect. The team wheeled up in
fine style, and we found the change of horses ready harnessed and supper waiting. Mr. Shackleford assured us
that he would have fired a gun for us, but he could not
get it to go off. We took the will for the deed, however,
and hustled in to supper, which was soon despatched.
After taking leave of Mr. Corbin and the others, we were
off again to the next station, having been detained, in all,
twenty minutes.

This locality is called Syracuse,[26] and is principally
owned by T. R. Brayton and Mr. Shackleford, who have
done much to establish the route through this section. The
Pacific Railroad Company is now building a depot here,
and the western terminus will shortly be extended to it.[27] I
should have mentioned before that it is in Morgan County.
From this point I considered myself fairly under way in
the coaches, and must confess that I felt quite as fatigued
with the first few miles as with as many hundred which I

[26] Platted in 1858 as Pacific City, and renamed in the same year after
Syracuse, N.Y. See D. W. Eaton, "How Missouri Counties, Towns, and
Streams Were Named," *Mo. Hist. Rev.*, XI, 335.

[27] The railroad reached Syracuse Aug. 1, 1859. See Jennings, pp. 308-9.

have travelled since. The change from railroad to coach travelling is somewhat marked, though one of our party very justly observed that on the Pacific road the change is so gradual as to be hardly perceptible. I do think that road quite equal to that monument of human enterprise, the Long Island Railroad, though generally, I must admit, I found the western railroads very well managed.

As the road to the next station, though only thirteen miles, was nearly all up hill, we were one hour and forty-five minutes in reaching it[28]—which was considered pretty good time. Our horses were four in number, that being the allotment all along the line from Tipton to San Francisco. They were ready and harnessed at this point, and to change teams was the work of but a few minutes, and we were off again. This time we got a driver who was sick, and the road being somewhat bad made our progress slow, and the sixteen miles to Burns' occupied three hours. The driver from here did not know the road well, and we had to feel our way along, as the night was dark, the roads very difficult, and the coach lamps seemed to be of little use in the dim moonlight; and the sixteen miles to Warsaw[29] on the Osage River occupied another three hours. Yet, though this might appear to be slow travelling, it was even faster than required by the time table. As we

[28] Mulholland's station. Supplied names of stations are from G. Bailey's report appended to "Report of the Postmaster General" for 1858, in *The Executive Documents, Printed by Order of the Senate of the United States, Second Session, Thirty-fifth Congress, 1858-'59* (Washington, 1859), IV, No. 1, pt. 4, pp. 739-44. Bailey, a special agent of the Post Office Department, traveled on the first eastbound stage.

[29] The county seat of Benton County; platted in 1837, and in 1838 named after the capital of Poland. See Eaton, in *Mo. Hist. Rev.*, X, 209.

neared the stations we blew our horns to apprise them of our coming.

At Warsaw, though we arrived about three A.M., and ahead of time, we found our horses ready harnessed, and were soon on our way to the next station, eleven miles distant.[30] The road led through a ford of the Osage River and a dense forest, full of rocky hills, and the night was now dark as pitch. As we left Warsaw we had to be preceded by a man on horseback, with a light to show us the way through the ford, but the river being rather low there was not much danger. I began to feel some fear of wet feet and mail bags when the water reached the hub, but we got over safely and pretty dry, as the water was not deeper than half the wheels. We made the eleven miles in two hours, and I must confess it was a matter of the utmost astonishment to me how the driver ever found his way in the wilderness. We went "right along about east," as young John said, and much to the fear of the old gentleman that we would upset.

The next ten miles was made in an hour and a half, bringing us to Quincy,[31] where we took breakfast. Fourteen miles through the prairies brought us to Youst,[32] in an hour and forty minutes; sixteen miles to Bolivar,[33] in two hours and twenty minutes; eleven miles to Smith's, in one hour and four minutes; and twenty miles to Spring-

[30] Bailey's station.

[31] Platted in 1848, in Hickory County. See Eaton, in *Mo. Hist. Rev.*, XI, 173.

[32] Bailey spells this Yost.

[33] The county seat of Polk County, which was organized in 1835. The town was named after Bolivar, Tenn., which in turn was named after Simon Bolivar. See Eaton, in *Mo. Hist. Rev.*, XI, 342.

field,[34] in three hours and five minutes—which made it just a quarter past three o'clock on Friday, when we were not required by the time table to leave the place until a quarter to eight on Saturday. The ride was, though rather fatiguing to a novitiate, rather pleasant on the whole. The views of the little prairies, the vast fields of corn, tobacco, and wild mustard seed, the picturesque encampment of the "travellers," the fields of Chinese sugar cane, droves of roving cattle, the sounding of merry horns as we approached the stations, the bustle of changing horses, and the entire novelty of the scene, made an impression upon my mind which will never be effaced.

I can never forget the grotesque figures which my imagination conjured up out of the objects in the woods on our first night out. The stories I had read of bands of roving Indians, rambling through the forests but to kill and steal, all rushed to my mind, and transformed each decayed tree or stunted bush into a lurking foe. Then, the music of the forest, the moonlight struggling through the trees, the easy motion of the vehicle as it rocked to and fro on the rough road, like a vessel moving on the sea, all tended to make one thoughtful of the impressiveness of the occasion. Young John enlivened the road with his eagerness to get on and to make good time, and evinced the greatest anxiety that no accident should happen to interfere with the safe carriage of the mail. There seemed to be a sort of catching enthusiasm about the whole trip, which excited more interest—I know for myself—than I ever supposed could be mustered out of the bare fact of a common coach travelling over a common road, with a

[34] The county seat of Greene County, platted in 1835, and named after Springfield, Tenn. See Eaton, in *Mo. Hist. Rev.*, XI, 170.

common mail bag and a few common people inside. But
the occasion made them all uncommon, and I soon got so
that I would willingly go without my dinner for the privilege of helping along that mail a quarter of an hour. Indeed, we did do this on our way to Springfield, when Mr.
Butterfield got up a temporary lunch for us as the coach
stopped alongside of a spring, and we took a nice social
meal in its shade.

I forget, now, what county Springfield is in, but you
can easily find it by looking along the central part of
western Missouri, and bringing your eye on the line of
the source of her many small rivers. It is a flourishing
town, of about two thousand inhabitants, and has been for
twenty-five years the seat of the General Land Office. It
has several churches, a branch of the State Bank of Missouri, and if somebody there had enterprise enough to
build a lot of houses it would be a rapidly growing town.
The passage through it of the overland mail, and the establishment of a daily line to connect with the railroad for
St. Louis, have much increased its importance. As our
team drove up to the door there was quite an excitement raised in the town, and the people all gathered round
to see the first overland mail, congratulating both the But-
terfields on the occasion. The time made from Tipton to
Springfield was the quickest ever before made, owing to
the promptness with which the relays of horses were procured; and had it not been for accidents, before spoken
of, it would have been made in even quicker time. Every
one conceded that the overland mail had done remarkably
well, and pretty soon our arrival was honored with a
salute of several guns.

Our stay was just long enough to change from the coach

to one of the wagons, such as are used from this point to San Francisco. They are made much like the express wagons in your city which carry goods for transhipment, only they are heavier built, have tops made of canvass, and are set on leather straps instead of springs. Each one has three seats, which are arranged so that the backs let down and form one bed, capable of accommodating from four to ten persons, according to their size and how they lie. I found it a very agreeable bed for one, afterwards. Everything being in readiness, we got started again at four o'clock, having been detained at Springfield three-quarters of an hour. We drove off to the post office and took on a small through mail for San Francisco, and also the postmaster and another citizen, who wished to have it to say that they had ridden in the first coach from Springfield containing the overland mail. It was gratifying to me, as one of the few evidences of interest in the enterprise which we met. One thing struck me as creditable, and that was that the mail bag from Springfield was quite as large as that from St. Louis.

We kept travelling all day and night, of course, our way during Friday afternoon and evening being through an extremely dusty, hilly, and stony road, as will appear when I state the fact that the first fourteen miles took two hours; the next twenty, three hours; the next fifteen, two hours and forty-five minutes; the next seventeen, three hours; and the next eighteen, three hours and twenty minutes.[35] This brought us to breakfast time on Saturday morning, at Callahan's, but about twelve miles from Fayetteville, Arkansas, very near the border line. Here we found Mr. Crocker, the superintendent of the line between

[35] The stations were Ashmore's, Smith's, Couch's, and Harburn's, respectively.

St. Louis and Memphis and Fort Smith, Arkansas, where the two mails converge and proceed together. We greased our wagon, changed horses, and got some breakfast—all in an incredibly short space of time—after which we set out for Fayetteville.

The route leads over those steep and rugged hills which surround the Ozark range in this section of Arkansas, and we were just three hours going from Callahan's to Fayetteville.[36] This town is located up among the hills, in a most inaccessible spot, in Franklin County,[37] said by its inhabitants to be the star county of the state. It has two churches, the county court house, a number of fine stores and dwellings, and, I believe, about 1,800 inhabitants. It is a flourishing little town, and its deficiency of a good hotel will, I understand, be supplied by Mr. Butterfield, who has bought some property for that purpose. He is the most energetic president of a company I ever saw. He appears to know every foot of the ground and to be known by everybody, while his son John has been very active in getting good stock on this end of the route, in which, I think, he has succeeded.

We made a small addition to our mail here, and at just ten minutes to twelve started for Fort Smith, on the border line between Arkansas and Indian Territory, and about sixty-five miles distant. We started at ten minutes to twelve on Saturday, when the time table only required us to start at a quarter past ten on Sunday—so we were at this point twenty-two hours and seventeen minutes ahead of time as set down in the time table by which the Post Office De-

[36] Bailey records a Fitzgerald's station between Callahan's (which he spells Callaghan's) and Fayetteville.

[37] Should read Washington County.

partment required us to run—this, too, in spite of the one or two little annoyances referred to, and a pretty heavy load of baggage and passengers which had not been expected. It could only have been accomplished by the most perfect arrangement for, and promptness in, the relays of horses and the excellence of the stock purchased. We had now gone two hundred and forty-three miles, through, I think, some of the roughest part of the country on the route, and yet gained time. I must confess that I began to get quite enthusiastic on the subject of the mail myself, and looked upon the mail bags and the horses with quite as much interest as I should have had in the Atlantic cable had I been on that world renowned expedition. I jumped out and got water for the horses, kept an eye on the mail bags, walked up the steep hills, and forgot the terrible pain in the back which such incessant riding without sleep occasioned.

We have now arrived at Colheet's [Colbert's] Ferry on the Red River, about eight miles below Preston, on the Texas border; we are just thirty-five hours ahead of the time table. An express is just leaving us for Fort Smith, and as I wish to send this I must cut off my letter without the most interesting portion—our reception at Fort Smith, meeting the Memphis mail, journey through the Indian Territory, and arrival here today at about ten o'clock. I must send this and take my chance to send the rest. I have one comfort, at any rate: the *Herald* will have the exclusive news, and I can wait with a better grace. We have the strongest hopes of reaching San Francisco in less than the twenty-five days. I find roughing it on the plains agrees with me, so that I guess I could go without eating or sleeping for a week. I hope I shan't have to try it, though.

New York Herald, Sunday, October 24, 1858

The Overland Mail

Our Special Overland Correspondence
Overland Mail Wagon, near Fort Belknap,
Young Co., Texas, Sept. 22, 1858

*The Route from Fayetteville to Fort Smith. Difficulties of the
Ozark Range. Magnificence of the Mountain Scenery. The
Choctaw Reservation. Condition of the Negroes among the
Indian Slaveholders. A Visit to Governor Walker. Accidents
of the Road. Dreams and Realities, &c., &c.*

MY LAST letter left the overland mail en route from
Fayetteville, Arkansas, to Fort Smith, Arkansas. Since
then we have passed through the Indian Territory, crossing the Red River at Colbert's Ferry, through Grayson,
Cooke, Montague, Wise, and Young counties, Texas, to
Fort Belknap, and are now on our way to Fort Chadbourne, from whence I expect to send this; and when we
reach there we shall have gone 945 miles on our journey.

Fayetteville is in Franklin County,[38] Arkansas, among

[38] Should read **Washington County.**

the hills of the Ozark range of mountains. We left there on Saturday, the 18th inst., at two minutes before noon —just twenty-two hours and thirteen minutes ahead of the time required of us by the time table. Even among these hills you do not lose sight of the prairie nature of the West; for just after leaving Fayetteville you see a fine plain, surrounded with hills—in fact, a prairie in the mountains. After a rather rough ride of fourteen miles, which we accomplished with our excellent team in one hour and three-quarters, we took a team of four mules[39] to cross the much dreaded Ozark range, including the Boston Mountain. I had thought before we reached this point that the rough roads of Missouri and Arkansas could not be equalled; but here Arkansas fairly beats itself.

I might say our road was steep, rugged, jagged, rough, and mountainous—and then wish for some more expressive words in the language. Had not Mr. Crocker provided a most extraordinary team I doubt whether we should have been able to cross in less than two days. The wiry, light, little animals tugged and pulled as if they would tear themselves to pieces, and our heavy wagon bounded along the crags as if it would be shaken in pieces every minute, and ourselves disembowelled on the spot. For fifteen miles the road winds among these mountains at a height of nearly two thousand feet above the Gulf of Mexico. The approach to it from Fayetteville is through a pleasant and fertile valley; and I understand that these valleys comprise some of the best agricultural districts of Arkansas. The mountains abound in splendid white oak timber. As the road winds along the ridges you are afforded most magnificent views of the surrounding hills and valleys

[39] At Park's station.

—especially in the winter, when the foliage is less an obstruction than it was when we passed over. But we had a clear day, and I can only say that our mountain views in the Highlands of the Hudson are but children's toys in comparison with these vast works of nature.

The term "Boston Mountain" is, I believe, derived from a prevailing western fashion of applying that name to anything which is considered very difficult. But Connecticut hills and roads are mere pimples and sandpaper compared with the Ozark ranges. By hard tugging we got up, and with the aid of brakes and drags we got down; and I can assure you we were by no means sorry when that herculean feat was accomplished. The mules which took us over the mountains carried us, in all, about nineteen miles, when we took another team of horses to carry us to Fort Smith.[40]

We crossed the Arkansas, in a flatboat much resembling a raft, at Van Buren,[41] a flourishing little town on its banks. Our course through the soft bed of the flats (which were not covered, owing to the low state of the river) was somewhat hazardous, as our heavy load was liable to be sunk on the quicksands which abound here. But by the aid of a guide on horseback, with a lantern (for it was night), we crossed the flats, and up the steep sandy bank in safety. Picking our way cautiously for five or six miles, we reached Fort Smith on the Arkansas River, just on the border of Arkansas and the Indian Territory, at five min-

[40] According to Bailey's report this would be Brodie's station; he also records a Woosley's station, located between Brodie's and Fort Smith.

[41] First known as Phillip's Landing. It was named after Martin Van Buren, in 1836, and later became the county seat of Crawford County. See *Centennial History*, ed. Herndon, I, 884-85.

utes after two o'clock A.M., having made the sixty-five miles from Fayetteville in fourteen hours and seven minutes, or three hours and seven minutes less than schedule time. We had anticipated beating the mail which left Memphis, Tenn., on the 16th to meet us at Fort Smith, several hours; but as soon as we entered the town, though at so unseasonable an hour, we found it in a great state of excitement on account of the arrival of the Memphis mail just fifteen minutes before us. But, though they had 700 miles to travel, five hundred of them were by steamboat, from Memphis to Little Rock,[42] and it was said that they got their mails before we did.

Fort Smith[43] is a thriving town of about 2,500 inhabitants, and they boast that every house is full. There are two newspapers, both of which were, I believe, started by Judge Wheeler, who was a passenger by the overland mail route from St. Louis. As several other routes over the plains pass through this place, and have contributed much to its growth, the people evinced much interest; and the news that both the St. Louis and Memphis stages had arrived spread like wildfire. Horns were blown, houses were lit up, and many flocked to the hotel to have a look at the wagons and talk over the exciting topic, and have a peep at the first mail bags. The general interest was so contagious that I, though I had but a few minutes to spare before the stage started again, actually employed the time in writing ten lines to my wife instead of the *Herald*. I

[42] A contemporary account by a passenger over the Memphis route is reprinted in the Appendix.

[43] Established as an army post in 1817, first called Belle Point, and later named Fort Smith after General Thomas A. Smith, who was commanding the Ninth Military Department. The town was incorporated in 1842. See *Centennial History*, ed. Herndon, I, 847-58.

must say, however, that I expected you would hear of the few facts I could then communicate, before a letter from me could reach you, by means of the telegraph.

An hour and twenty-five minutes was consumed in examining the way mails, arranging the way bill, joining the two mails from Memphis and St. Louis, and changing stages; and precisely at half-past three A.M. on Sunday, the 19th inst., the stage left Fort Smith, being exactly twenty-four hours ahead of the time required in the time table, which had been gained in the first four hundred and sixty-eight miles of our journey. I was the only person in the wagon which left Fort Smith—beside Mr. Fox, the mail agent, and the driver. Mr. John Butterfield, the president of the Overland Mail Company, had accompanied us thus far, and, though sixty-five years of age,[44] had borne the fatiguing, sleepless journey as well, if not better, than any of the rest. Indeed, I felt ashamed to complain when I saw one of his years stand out so well. Certainly, if the overland mail does not succeed, it will not be for lack of his arduous personal exertions. He urged the men in changing horses at every station, often taking hold to help, and on one occasion driving for a short distance. He is, however, an old stager, and is in his element in carrying on this enterprise. I cannot be too grateful to him, on your behalf, as well as my own, for the kind facilities which he extended to me.

We forded the Arkansas at Fort Smith, and for the first time since our departure from St. Louis I had an opportunity to sleep in the wagon, wrapped up in blankets and stretched on the seats. It took some time to get accustomed to the jolting over the rough road, the rocks, and

[44] Actually, Butterfield was only fifty-seven.

log bridges; but three days' steady riding without sleep helped me in getting used to it, and I was quite oblivious from the time of crossing the Arkansas to the first stopping place in the Indian Territory, about sixteen miles from the river, which we reached about daylight. Here is a large farm owned by an Indian and worked by a white man from the East. I here saw several friendly Choctaws on their way east.

The Choctaw reservation extends through the south-eastern portion of the Indian Territory, and the Indians are to be met all along the road, either travelling or located in their log huts. Many of them are quite wealthy, their property consisting chiefly in cattle and Negroes. Their ownership of slaves is quite common, and many of them have large numbers. In their treatment of them they are generally more lenient than the white slaveholders, and appear to let them do pretty much as they please. I noticed in riding through the territory but little farming going on. The fact is, but little land is worked. Though the soil is well adapted for producing corn, tobacco, hemp, &c., they generally prefer to raise stock. They brand their cattle and let them run on the plains, which during nine months of the year yield excellent pasturage. During the remaining three months they generally get poor, having only the winter grass of the creeks to subsist upon.

Many of the Choctaws own large herds of cattle, and live well on the increase. Their habitations are mostly off the road. Those on the road appear to be the most miserable specimens of the western log hut, and many of them are deserted. As we rode along we could see them lazily basking in the sun or reclining in the cool porticos, which are built, in most of the huts, so as to divide the house in the centre, affording a very pleasant location for dining or sitting in warm weather. What struck me forcibly was the squalid misery which seemed to characterize most of them—which was only surpassed by the appearance of their Negroes, with whom, I am told, they often co-habit. They generally shrugged their shoulders as the stage passed, but seldom said anything beyond "Good day"—and only that when spoken to.

About seventeen miles from the crossing of the Arkansas we came to the residence of Governor Wm. Walker, the governor of the territory.[45] He looks like a full-blooded white man, though I understand he has some Indian blood in his veins. His wife is a half-breed Indian of the Choc-taw Nation. He was elected at the last election and has held his office but about six months. The salary is one thousand dollars per year. He has a farm of several hun-dred acres, a very comfortable house, and owns several hundred head of cattle. The place is called Scullyville [Skullyville], and his house is made a station for changing horses.[46] In personal appearance he looks like a well-to-do farmer. On this occasion he came out in his shirt sleeves and helped hitch the horses. He has considerable influence with the Nation, and is favorably disposed toward the Overland Mail Company.

[45] Tandy C. (not William) Walker, who died in 1877, was president of the senate of the general council of the Choctaw Nation, assuming the duties of governor when Alfred Wade, who had been elected governor under the Skullyville constitution of 1857, resigned on Jan. 12, 1858. See Grant Foreman, "The California Overland Mail Route through Oklahoma," *Chronicles of Oklahoma*, IX, 307 n.; W. B. Morrison, "The Saga of Skully-ville," *ibid.*, XVI, 238-40.

[46] Skullyville was established, about 1832, as an Indian agency. Walker's house was the old agency house where government annuities were paid to Indian expatriates. See M. H. Wright, "Historic Places on the Old Stage Line from Fort Smith to Red River," *ibid.*, XI, 810; Morrison, *ibid.*, XVI, 234-40.

Though, by the laws of the Nation, an Indian may procure a divorce at pleasure upon the payment of ten dollars, there is one provision which I think our strong minded women will approve of, and that is that the wife is entitled to half the property. This provision is rigidly adhered to, and husband and wife are quite as strict in their dealings with each other as with others. Most of the Choctaws speak our language, though for purposes of mere civility; they do not care much about using it. The bane of the Choctaws, as well as of many white nations, is the use of intoxicating liquors, which they will procure in spite of all precautions. The laws of the territory make it an offence, punishable by fine and imprisonment, to give or sell liquor to an Indian; but they will drink camphene, burning fluid, or "Perry Davis' Pain Killer," or the whole three mixed, for the purpose of getting drunk, and when in that state their performances are said to be not less remarkable than those of their white brethren in the same condition. They are generally quite averse to work, and it is with the greatest difficulty that they can be compelled to do their portion toward mending the road.

From the Arkansas River to Scullyville [Skullyville] there appeared to be considerable land under cultivation, but as we proceeded there was less to be seen. The land is well watered, and with little cultivation could be made to yield abundantly; but they prefer to let their stock grow and increase without their care, and draw their small pensions from the government. The Indians we saw along the road looked squalid and miserable generally, though occasionally we met some very fine specimens of the red men of the forest. These, however, were mostly half-breeds, who are by far the most enterprising and industrious, and

avail themselves of the education fund to educate their
children. This fund, I believe, amounts to $10,000, and
is amply sufficient for its purpose.[47] The Chickasaws, who
occupy a more westerly reservation, are much more advanced in civilization than the Choctaws.

After leaving Gov. Walker's the next station (sixteen
miles distant) was reached in about two hours and a half,
and two other stations, at about equal distances, in about
the same time each.[48] I took my breakfast and dinner out
of a provision basket which had been kindly placed in the
wagon by the forethought of Mr. Butterfield, who had
not forgotten the needful with which to wash it down.
Though it consisted of but a few cold cuts, my memory
still clings to it as the last civilized meal between Fort
Smith and the barren plains where I now write. I have
said nothing of the homely meals provided on the way
from Tipton to Fort Smith, for I considered them as but
the well known accompaniments of Hoosier life; but, ever
since I left that last meal of cold ham, cakes, crackers, and
cheese, fond recollection recalls it to view. Though I am
no epicurean, I could not forbear writing its obituary.

About fifty miles from the Arkansas River, on our road,
I noticed the first plain, or prairie, of consequence in the
Indian Territory. It was a rolling plain, I should judge
full twenty miles in circumference. The soil looked so
black and rich that I was surprised to see so little verdure,

[47] The amount appropriated by the Choctaw Nation for the school year
1858-59 was about $22,000, which does not include contributions made by
the various missionary boards under whose auspices the schools operated.
See *Report of the Commissioner of Indian Affairs . . . for the Year 1859*
(Washington, 1860), pp. 187-207.

[48] Trahern's, Holloway's, and Riddle's stations, respectively.

A full account, with a good map, of the overland mail route through the
Indian Territory is to be found in Wright, in *Chron. of Okla.*, XI, 798-822.

but I soon learned that this color was caused by the grass having been set on fire. On the western border, Mr. Mc-Donnell, the mail agent, pointed out to me a curious ledge of black sandstone rocks, which had very much the appearance of the ruins of a large building, so regularly were they laid. As we proceeded west, the country which had before—at least on our road—been of a forest nature, grew more open, and the rolling plains and smoother roads grew more frequent. We soon met many bands of Choctaw Indians in charge of large herds of cattle. They never took any more notice of us than to look pretty sharply at us and to say good day if spoken to. We also met many emigrants from Texas in their covered wagons containing their families and all their wordly possessions, camping at night and luxuriating on their dried beef, coffee, and perhaps corn from the nearest cornfield.

At Pussey [Pusley] (a station for changing horses, where an Indian of that name lives), about sixty-six miles from the river, I met an old Indian who owns seven hundred head of cattle, and a pretty daughter, and is willing to give the half of the one to the white man who will marry the other. Here I gave an Indian boy a paper of tobacco to give me water enough to wash my face, put on a blue flannel shirt, and considered myself pretty well on my way out West.

In the little plains which we passed, we frequently saw the tall posts which the Indians use in playing ball. The players divide themselves into two parties, one standing at each post. The throwers aim to hit the posts, and the catchers must capture the ball in little bowls with which each is provided, a penalty being inflicted for catching the ball with the hands. They become very much excited at this game, and gamble with it very often.[49]

From the night of Thursday, the 16th, up to the night of Sunday, the 19th, I had travelled continuously without accident, both night and day, and at a pretty rapid rate. On Sunday night, when within a few miles of Blackburn's station (which is about sixty miles from Red River), I thought all hopes of a quick trip for the first overland mail were at an end. We had taken a splendid team of horses at the last station, and had been spinning over the rolling prairies at a rapid rate; our route for some hours had been over these hills with their gradual elevations, and our driver had urged his team pretty well. We now came to a patch of woods through which the road was tortuous and stony. But our driver's ambition to make good time overcame his caution, and away we went, bounding over the stones at a fearful rate.

The moon shone brightly, but its light was obstructed by the trees, and the driver had to rely much on his knowledge of the road for a guide. To see the heavy mail wagon whizzing and whirling over the jagged rock, through such a labyrinth, in comparative darkness, and to feel oneself bouncing—now on the hard seat, now against the roof, and now against the side of the wagon—was no joke, I assure you, though I can truthfully say that I rather liked the excitement of the thing. But it was too dangerous to be continued without accident, and soon two heavy thumps and a bound of the wagon that unseated us all, and a crashing sound, denoted that something had broken. We

[49] For descriptions of variations of this game, called in Choctaw "Ishtaboli," see J. R. Swanton, *Source Material for the Social and Ceremonial Life of the Choctaw Indians* (Smithsonian Institution, Bureau of American Ethnology, *Bulletin*, No. 103; Washington, 1931), pp. 140-55.

stopped and examined, but found no damage except a broken seat, and proceeded to the station. Here a further examination, to our utter astonishment, disclosed the fact that the pole, or tongue, of the wagon was badly split. It was a mystery to me how we ever reached the station without completing its destruction. It took more time to mend it than the ambitious driver saved. Moral—"Make haste slowly." After repairing damages we got started again, and travelled the next 18 miles in two hours and a quarter.

The night was beautifully clear and bright, and I was tempted to stay up and enjoy it; but I had become too much fatigued with the journey to be able to withstand the demands of somnolence, and, wrapping myself up in my shawls, was soon obliviously snoring on the extended seats of the wagon. I awoke but once during the night, having been jolted into a position where my neck felt as if there was a knot in it. They had stopped at a station[50] to change horses, and for the time not a sound could I hear. I had been dreaming of the Comanche Indians, and in the confusion of drowsiness first thought that the driver and the mail agent had been murdered, and that I, being covered up in the blankets, had been missed; then I recollected that I had a pistol and thought of feeling for it; but finally I thought I would not stir, for fear the Indians would see me—when I was brought to my senses by a familiar voice saying "Git up there, old hoss," and found it was the driver hitching up a new team.

During the night we went eighteen miles in two hours and a half. The next thirteen miles took three hours, owing to the bad state of the roads, bringing us to Garey's

[50] Waddell's station.

[Geary's] station. Mr. Garey [Geary] has a hundred acres of corn, which is considered a pretty fair lot for this section of the country. Another ride of seventeen miles occupied but two hours and a half, bringing us to the "Boggy Depot," where there are several painted houses and a few stores.[51] I learned that near here, a few days since, an Indian got shot while in a quarrel about politics —for you must know that the old Wigwam at Tammany is not the only spot where the braves settle political questions with hard knocks. The Nation is divided on the question of forming a state government. The two parties wax strong on their respective sides, and frequent collisions are the consequence. I do not wish to be unfair on the subject, but I am given to understand that the half-breeds and whites and more intelligent full-bloods are in favor of the state government.

Fourteen miles from Boggy Depot we came to Blue River station,[52] where a very heavy bridge is building for the company. Here I saw a copy of the *Weekly Herald*— a distance of six hundred miles from St. Louis, and nearly seventeen hundred from New York overland, and twenty-five miles from any post office. I thought the *Herald* was appreciated there.

A ride of three hours brought us to Colbert's Ferry on the Red River—the boundary between Texas and the Indian Territory. We arrived here on Monday, the 20th

[51] Boggy Depot's first building was erected in 1837, and the town, which was located about a mile west of the Clear Boggy River, was officially named when a post office was established in 1849. "Boggy" is a translation of the name given to the river by the eighteenth-century French traders, who called it "Vazzures," from the word "vaseux," meaning miry or boggy. See M. H. Wright, "Old Boggy Depot," *Chron. of Okla.*, V, 4-6.

[52] Located at Nail's crossing. Between this station and the next one mentioned by Ormsby—Colbert's Ferry—was Fisher's Stand.

inst., at ten minutes to ten—being, altogether, thirty-four hours ahead of time to this point. But here was a difficulty. There was no team to carry on the mail. Arrangements had been made to put it through in quick time on the regular day, but it was not expected a day and a half in advance. Indeed, there was nothing left to do but to put up with it. We had, by several mere accidents, been enabled to obtain our relays so far in advance, and now we could afford a little loss of time. We had a good dinner, and I took advantage of the opportunity to write to you— the first chance off the wagon since Thursday, the 16th.

Mr. Colbert, the owner of the station and of the ferry, is a half-breed Indian of great sagacity and business tact. He is a young man—not quite thirty, I should judge—and has a white wife—his third. He has owned and run this ferry five years, and has had excellent patronage, from its central location, being about midway between Preston and the one below.[53]

Mr. Colbert evinces some enterprise in carrying the stages of the company across his ferry free of charge, in consideration of the increased travel which it will bring his way. He also stipulates to keep the neighboring roads in excellent order, and has already done much towards it. He has a large gang of slaves at work on the banks of the river, cutting away the sand, so as to make the ascent easy.

[53] Benjamin Franklin Colbert (1828-93), the son of Chickasaw parents, was born in Chickasaw country, near Horn Lake, Miss. He located on the Red River in the early forties, and became one of the wealthiest citizens in the Nation. In 1858 the Chickasaw legislature granted him the privilege of establishing a ferry across the Red River. Colbert was married four times, in all, and was the father of fourteen children. See Wright, in *Chron. of Okla.*, XI, 812-13; W. B. Morrison, "Colbert Ferry on Red River, Chickasaw Nation, Indian Territory: Recollections of John Malcolm, Pioneer Ferryman," *ibid.*, XVI, 305 n.

His boat is simply a sort of raft, pushed across the shallow stream by the aid of poles in the hands of sturdy slaves. The fare for a four-horse team is a dollar and a quarter, and the net revenue of the ferry about $1,000 per annum. He thinks of either buying a horse boat or having a stout cable drawn across the river, so that one man could manage the boat. I suggested to him to buy a piece of the Atlantic cable, but he was of the opinion that it would be too costly. He owns about twenty-five slaves, and says he considers them about the best stock there is, as his increase is about four per year. He has a fine farm, and raises considerable corn—how much I do not know. At his table I saw sugar, butter, and pastry—the first two of which have been exceedingly rare articles since I left Fort Smith, and the last of which I have not seen anywhere else since I left Fort Smith. He is nearly white, very jovial and pleasant, and, altogether, a very good specimen of the half-breed Indian.

We had determined, after giving our horses a brief rest, to proceed with them until we met the other team coming back from Sherman; but just as we were about starting with them the expected team rode up, and all haste was made for our departure over Colbert's Ferry into Texas. We crossed the wide, shallow, and muddy Red River on one of Mr. Colbert's boats, and saw quite a large number of his slaves busily engaged in lowering the present steep grade up the banks. He also undertakes to keep in order part of the road on the Texas side of the river. On our way to Sherman in Texas, we passed several large gullies, or beds of creeks, which are being bridged at the expense of Grayson County, in which Sherman is situated and of which it is the county seat.

Sherman[54] is a pleasant little village of about six hundred inhabitants, and is noted for its enterprising citizens. We found Mr. Bates, the superintendent of this part of the line, ready with a team of mules to carry the mail on without a moment's delay. As soon as we drove up, our teams were unhitched and new ones put in their places at short notice. But Mr. Bates objected to a heavy load of ammunition which was in our wagon, as too much of an incumbrance for the mail, and in a twinkling another wagon was rolled out and we were started on our way. I had barely time to run a few steps to the post office to drop you a letter.

The time of our departure was twenty minutes to 5 P.M. on Monday, the 20th of September—four days, six hours, and twenty minutes from the time of our departure from St. Louis, a distance of six hundred and seventy-three miles, and we had travelled but one hundred and sixty by railroad, and were thirty-one hours and fifty minutes ahead of time.

Overland Mail Wagon, near El Paso, Texas
Sept. 28, 1858

Meeting of the Eastern and Western Overland Mails. Progress from Colbert's Ferry. Pope's Camp. Table of Time Made from St. Louis to the Pecos River, &c., &c.

The overland mail from St. Louis and Memphis to San Francisco met the mail from San Francisco to each of

[54] Founded in 1848 and named in honor of Colonel Sidney Sherman, of San Jacinto fame.

For additional information concerning the stage line through Texas see W. A. Riney, "Retracing the Butterfield Trail," in West Tex. Hist. Assoc.

those places, this evening about half past eight, one hundred miles east of El Paso—eight hours ahead of time. The mail going west was due at El Paso (1,308 miles from St. Louis), on Tuesday, the 28th inst., at 11 A.M., and the mail going east was due at the same place (1,332½ miles from San Francisco) on the same day at 5:30 A.M. So you will perceive that the mail going east has rather beaten the mail going west, so far, though they may lose time in going over the remaining route.

I have already given you a hasty sketch of our progress from St. Louis, via the Pacific Railroad, to Tipton, Moniteau County, Mo., thence to Springfield, Mo., Fayetteville and Fort Smith, Arkansas, the Indian Territory to the Texas border, and our start from Sherman, Texas—having crossed the Red River at Colbert's Ferry about eight miles below Fort Preston. Since then we have passed through Gainesville, Forts Belknap and Chadbourne, along the Concho River—a branch of the little Colorado—to its source, across the great Llano Estacado or Stake[d] Plain —a distance of eighty miles without water—to the Horsehead Crossing of the Pecos River, and up the east bank of that stream to Pope's Camp, crossing the Pecos about three miles above, and taking the line near the thirty-second parallel for El Paso. We travel night and day, and only stop long enough to change teams and eat. The stations are not all yet finished, and there are some very long drives—varying from thirty-five to seventy-five miles —without an opportunity of procuring fresh teams. Many

Year Book, IX (Oct., 1933), 97-100; R. C. Crane, "Stage-Coaching in the Concho Country," *ibid.*, X (Oct., 1934), 58-67; R. N. Richardson, "Some Details of the Southern Overland Mail," *The Southwestern Historical Quarterly*, XXIX, 1-18.

obstacles have been overcome, and I am sanguine of the ultimate success of the enterprise, however much I may now doubt its efficiency as an expeditious mail or available passenger route. I continue my narrative as far as possible.

The following table will show the time table, time for leaving, the various time table stations which we have passed, and the time when we actually left:

Place	Time Table—Time of Leaving	Actual Time of Leaving
St. Louis, Mo., and Memphis, Tenn.	Sept. 16, 8 A.M.	Sept. 16, 8 A.M.
Springfield, Mo.	Sept. 18, 7:45 A.M.	Sept. 17, 4 P.M.
Fayetteville [Ark.]	Sept. 19, 10:15 A.M.	Sept. 18, 12 M.
Fort Smith, Ark.	Sept. 20, 3:30 A.M.	Sept. 19, 3:30 A.M.
Sherman, Texas	Sept. 22, 12:30 A.M.	Sept. 20, 4:40 P.M.
Fort Belknap, do.	Sept. 23, 9 A.M.	Sept. 22, 7 A.M.
Fort Chadbourn[e], do.	Sept. 24, 3:15 P.M.	Sept. 23, 7 P.M.
Pecos Riv., do. (Em. C.)	Sept. 26, 3:45 A.M.	————

We did not cross at Emigrant Crossing.

The Overland Route to the Pacific

Special Correspondence of the Herald
Tucson, Arizona, Oct. 2, 1858

*The First Overland Mail from St. Louis Arrived at Tucson.
Murder of Americans. Description of the Route from Red River
to the Great Staked Plain. Taming Wild Mules. New Roads.
"Roughing It." Phantom Hill. Military Posts. Accidents and
Incidents. No Trouble from the Indians. Horrible Murders by
Mexicans, &c., &c.*

THE first overland mail from St. Louis and Memphis arrived here this evening at half past eight, but thirty-one
hours behind time, having made up twelve of the forty-

three hours behind at Franklin, opposite El Paso. We have had excellent weather, so far, and no accidents or troubles from the Indians. We are confident of reaching San Francisco within the twenty-five days. I send you the details of the trip as far as I have been able to complete them from the roughness of the roads. I have yet to give you the details of our journey across western Texas, the fertile valley of the Rio Grande, and the mountains of New Mexico.

Aside from the matters of interest along the route, the only news is of the murder of three Americans at Dragoon Springs, about seventy-five miles from here, by the Mexicans. The Americans were named James Burr, James Cunningham, and —— Lang. Mr. Silas B. St. John, of New York, narrowly escaped with his life by bravely defending himself. It appears that the Mexicans waited until the Americans were asleep and then attacked them with axes, killing the three almost instantly. They then attacked St. John, who defended himself with his pistol, though severely wounded, and drove them off. After they left he lay there three days and four nights, until the first mail from San Francisco came along—being then almost dead from his wounds, hunger, and thirst. He is now lying in the hospital at Fort Buchanan, and is likely to recover. All the parties were employed at the station by the mail company. It is supposed that the Mexicans designed to plunder the station, as when they escaped they took some property with them. A large reward has been offered for their apprehension.[55]

[55] The account of the fight and participants, as related by Ormsby, differs somewhat from St. John's version (recorded in T. E. Farish, *History of Arizona* [Phoenix, 1915], II, 1-10): In August, 1858, the company's road construction gang left St. John, with six men, to complete the

My previous letters have traced our course from St. Louis, through western Missouri, Arkansas, and the Indian territories, to the Red River border of Texas, at Colbert's Ferry, where we arrived thirty-five hours in advance of time-table time. Though the country through which we had passed was but sparsely peopled, it seemed like leaving home to bid farewell even to these settlements to proceed through the wilds of Texas, along its lonely plains and barren hills and dangerous frontier to the Rio Grande. The very log huts of the friendly Choctaws were like home in comparison to the almost uninhabited wilds which we were to traverse—where all the evidence of the presence of man was the faint trail of the teamsters. Up to this our progress had been quite rapid, as the distances between the stations were comparatively short, and our changes of teams were generally in readiness; but, in the unsettled country through which we were to pass, the stations were more irregular, less prepared and stocked with animals, and the roads by no means better, and we had yet to experience the beauties of waiting to tame wild

station at Dragoon Springs. The men were James Hughes, of Watertown, N.Y., James Laing, of Kentucky, William Cunningham, of Iowa, and three Mexican laborers, Guadalupe Ramirez, Pablo Ramirez (alias Chino), of Sonora, and Bonifacio Mirando, of Chihuahua. At midnight, Wednesday, Sept. 8, St. John changed the guard, posting Guadalupe for Laing. About one o'clock the Mexicans attacked the men, killing Hughes and severely wounding the other three. Cunningham died the following night. St. John and Laing were found, on Sunday, by Col. James B. Leach and the road party, who were on their way to California. Laing died Monday night. The assistant surgeon, B. J. D. Irwin, did not arrive from Fort Buchanan until Friday morning. St. John's arm was amputated, six days later he was moved to the fort, and three weeks afterward he mounted a horse and rode to Tucson. According to information supplied by Mr. John Davidson, curator of the Junipero Serra Museum, San Diego, St. John was born on Apr. 4, 1835, and died, in San Diego, on Sept. 15, 1919.

mules and "roughing it" on the road, so that all the time which we had gained was needed for the future.

As I told you in my last, we crossed the Red River at Colbert's Ferry, eight miles below Preston, and found many improvements on the road in progress on the Texas side of the river, under the liberal management of Grayson County, in which the flourishing town of Sherman is situated, and where we arrived on Monday afternoon, September 20. As we were now a day ahead of time, we should not have found teams in readiness had not an express been sent in advance to notify Mr. Bates, the superintendent between Sherman and Fort Chadbourne. His part of the road was so poorly stocked with animals, and those he had were so worn out in forwarding stuff for the other parts of the line, that he had to hire an extra team of mules, at short notice, to forward the mail to the next station, and these were pretty well tired from working all day. Most of his stock consisted of wild mules which had just been broken, and the process had not fitted them very well for carrying the mail with rapidity. Our extra team, however, took us along pretty fast.

We left Sherman at 4:40 P.M. on the 20th. Our course lay across a fine rolling prairie, covered with fine grass, but with no trees and scarcely a shrub for eighteen miles—crossing a number of beds of little brooks which were now dry, but whose banks in winter afford plentiful grazing for cattle, where rolling prairies thus intersected extend for sixty miles to the Lower Cross Timbers, a range of wide woodland extending, from the Red River to the Brazos, across this portion of Texas. The first station after leaving Sherman was twenty miles distant,[56] and our team

[56] Diamond's station.

travelled it in three hours, so that before we reached there the beautiful moonlight lit up the vast prairie, making its sameness appear like the boundless sea and its hills like the rolling waves.

Here we stopped and had the first opportunity of witnessing the operation of harnessing a wild mule. First he had to be secured with a laretto [*la reata*] round his neck, and drawn by main force to a tree or post; then the harness had to be put on piece by piece, care being taken to avoid his teeth and heels. Altogether, I should estimate the time consumed in the process at not less than half an hour to each wild mule, and that, when the mail has to wait for it, might, I think, much better be spent on the road. Indeed, I should quite as much deem it in accordance with the spirit of the age to see the mail wait for the leather of the mail bags or harness to be tanned. I was much amused with the process, but it seemed a little behind the age for the mail to wait for it, and no doubt when all the company's wild mules are tamed the mail will make better time.

Fortunately our express had hastened the preparations, so we were not long detained here, and made our next thirteen miles to Gainesville,[57] another flourishing little town, in good time. After hastily swallowing supper and changing horses, we were off again and made our next station in the woods, fifteen miles distant,[58] in two hours and ten minutes, Mr. Bates, who accompanied the mail, being determined to make the best possible time. At this

[57] The county seat of Cooke County; founded Aug. 19, 1850, and named after General Edmund Pendleton Gaines. See L. J. Wortham, *A History of Texas* (Fort Worth, 1924), V, 282-83.

[58] Davidson's station.

station there was nothing in readiness, the express rider having lost his way, and some detention was experienced in harnessing more wild mules.

Another disadvantage under which we labored, this trip, was that our road, for the most of the way, was nearly new, though Mr. Bates claims that from Sherman to Belknap at least forty miles are saved by it. It leads through the counties of Grayson, Cooke, Jacks [Jack], Montague, Wise, and Young, all of which contribute towards its expenses, and certainly it must be a favorite with some, for, though only opened one month before I passed over it, it was already pretty well marked with wagon tracks. There were very few heavy grades, and, with the combined efforts of the counties and the mail company, bids fair to become soon an excellent road. It must of course improve every day of its use.

Soon after leaving Gainesville we strike the Lower Cross Timbers, through which the new road runs for twenty miles. The trees grow wide apart, and are mainly of post oak. As I rode through them, the open spaces, absence of underbrush, and clean looking grass gave the entire wood the appearance of a vast orchard, and I could not get rid of the impression that there was plenty of fruit at hand. Just on the edge of the Lower Cross Timbers we came to a station[59] on the new road, where we had the first of a series of rough meals, which lasted for most of the remaining journey. The house was built of rough logs laid together roughly, and the chinks filled in with mud. The house was about twenty feet square, forming one room, and was occupied by two men keeping bache-

[59] Conolly's station.

lors' hall, as might well be judged from the condition of things, of which the reader may imagine.

Our arrival was unexpected, and there was some bustle in getting both breakfast and the team ready. The breakfast was served on the bottom of a candle box, and such as sat down were perched on inverted pails or nature's chair. There were no plates and but four tin cups for the coffee, which was served without milk or sugar. As there were six of us, including drivers and workmen, those not lucky enough to get a first cup had to wait for the second table. The edible—for there was but one—consisted of a kind of short cake, baked on the coals, each man breaking off his "chunk" and plastering on butter with his pocket knife; but butter is a rare luxury between the Red River and the Rio Grande—at least on this route at present—though doubtless it will be plenty when the line gets in running order so as to convey supplies to the stations. Such, nevertheless, was our meal here, and we were advised by the host to "hurry up before the chickens eat it"—which we did, to the no little discomfiture of the chickens. It tasted good to me, and I can assure you that it would doubtless taste as well to any one coming over the same route at the same rate of speed.

We rode the next twenty miles in four hours and twenty minutes,[60] over our new road, our course taking us through alternate plains and woods. These little plains, skirted with timber and appearing extremely fertile, seemed most inviting for the hand of the farmer, and promising to yield abundantly for the slightest labor. The frequency of these beautiful spots was quite remarkable during this

[60] Earhart's station.

ride; the woods seemed to alternate so regularly with these little plains I was quite sorry when we had passed them.

Another sixteen mile ride, occupying three hours and a half, brought us to Jacksborough [Jacksboro].[61] This town is in Jacks [Jack] County, and though but a year old contains a dozen houses and, I should judge, nearly two hundred inhabitants. It is on the edge of a large plain which, as we approached it, looked like a passive lake, so even and level was its surface; and one could easily imagine it to be a lake, with this town upon its borders. We took fresh mules, here, and rode all night through a rolling prairie country, studded with mesquite[62] timber—a sort of cross between the crab-apple and scrub oak and seldom larger than a respectable gooseberry bush.

Our mules were exceedingly stubborn and lazy during the night, and required the most constant urging to keep them on a respectable trot. It would seem to me that horses might be employed with both economy of time and labor, on this and many other portions of the route, though it is barely possible that the mules may do, with patience and hard work—both of which Mr. Bates seems willing to furnish. We arrived at Belknap on Wednesday, the 22d of September, at 5:25, in just four hours behind the time in which we should have made it, but still twenty-seven hours ahead of the time-table time—which, considering the mules, I thought was doing wonders for the first trip.[63]

Fort Belknap is on the Brazos River and is the county

[61] Jacksboro is the county seat.

[62] Ormsby invariably wrote "musquit" for mesquite.

[63] Bailey records a Murphy's station, located between Jacksboro and Fort Belknap.

seat of Young County, Texas, and also a frontier military station.[64] About two months since, the whole Second Regiment of cavalry was here encamped, but now there are only two companies of that regiment, under command of Major Thomas.[65] The town has about one hundred and fifty inhabitants, and the houses, most of them, look neat; there are several stores and a billiard saloon and post office. This was about the extent of my observation during our brief stay *in transitu*. I could not see the fort, being detained at a very good breakfast at the postmaster's house. The fort is not very formidable. As we left Belknap we crossed the Brazos River, fording it with ease, as the dirty red water was not deeper than an ordinary New York gutter. The river was, however, very low; but at times there is considerable water here and it has been known to be as deep as sixteen feet—so that the company contemplate establishing a ferry to provide against all possibilities.

Our course led us for forty miles through plains whose sterile plainness was only varied by clumps of black oaks or weeds and coarse grass, with hardly a house or field to beguile the dreary spectacle. The only objects of interest passed on the road were a train of government mules, a Comanche Indian woman riding "straddle," and herds of cattle taking care of themselves. This woman, by the way, was the only one of the blood-thirsty Comanche Nation

[64] Fort Belknap was established June 13, 1851, and was abandoned in Sept., 1867. It was located on the Red Fork of the Brazos River, eight miles above its junction with the Clear Fork. See T. H. S. Hamersly, *Complete Regular Army Register of the United States . . . 1779 to 1879* (3d ed.; Washington, 1881), Pt. II, p. 124. The county seat was moved to Graham in 1874. See West Tex. Hist. Assoc. *Year Book*, XII (July, 1936), 134-35.

[65] Major George Henry Thomas (1816-70) was one of the few officers in Texas at this time who, at the outbreak of the Civil War, did not join the Confederate army.

that I had the pleasure of seeing, though terrible tales are
told of their deeds of blood in this section of the country,
in the way of stealing stock and taking the scalps of strag-
gling travellers. Some of the settlers, here, say that these
acts of depredation are often committed by the Comanches
on the reservation, with arms furnished by our Indian
agents—while the northern Comanches get the credit
of it.

The Clear Fork of the Brazos was not very clear, but
even its muddy waters were a grateful boon for a bath
while our horses were being changed at the station on
the banks.⁶⁶ Here were in progress of erection a log hut
for the station keeper and help, and a corral, or yard, in
which to herd the mules and catch them for harnessing.
Dr. Birch, the mail agent, had everything in readiness, so
that I had to finish dressing in the wagon—so short was
the delay. They changed wagons, however, and took a
heavier loaded one—which I thought was bad policy.

Our next stopping place was at Smith's station, twenty-
three miles from Clear Fork, on the banks of a small creek.
No house had been built yet, those at the station living in
tents. They had nearly finished a fine corral for the stock,
making it of brush (as no timber could be had) and filling
in the chinks with mud. Our supper consisted of cake
cooked in the coals, clear coffee, and some dried beef
cooked in Mrs. Smith's best style. We changed horses or
mules and swallowed supper in double quick time and
were soon on our way again.

Our road from Clear Fork lay for a time through a
little valley, and wound among the hills almost on a level.

⁶⁶ Clear Fork station. Bailey records a Franz's station located between
Fort Belknap and Clear Fork.

On our left I noticed two bluffs whose position reminded me forcibly of East and West Rock as seen on entering New Haven harbor. But they were mere hills, as most of our road lay through rolling plains covered with good grass and mesquite timber—a sorry landscape, I assure you. Our way was, however, much enlivened by "Big Dick," our driver, who amused us with accounts of how he was three days "on the canal and never saw land, because he was drunk in the hold"—and various other things.

Our next stopping place was at Phantom Hill, a deserted military post, seventy-four miles from Fort Belknap and fifty-six from Chadbourne, on the road between the two. It was, I believe, built in 1851 or 1852, and after being occupied for some time was destroyed by fire by the soldiers in 1853, on the occasion of their being ordered to some other post. Over half a million dollars' worth of property was destroyed at the time; yet after a pretended investigation no conclusion was arrived at as to the cause of the diabolical deed. It was said that the officers and men were heartily disgusted with the station and wished to make certain of never going back; that, as they were leaving the fort, one of the principal officers was heard to say that he wished the place would burn down; and that the soldiers, taking him at his word, stayed behind and fired the buildings. Two things are pretty certain: first, that the soldiers did not like the place; and second, that, whether accidentally or not, it burned down just as they left it.[67]

[67] Officially designated as the Post on Clear Fork of the Brazos, but commonly called Fort Phantom Hill. It was established Nov. 14, 1851, and abandoned Apr. 6, 1854. See Hamersly, *op. cit.*, Pt. II, p. 125.

The cause of the destruction of the fort is a disputed point. See C. C. Rister, "The Border Post of Phantom Hill," in *West Tex. Hist. Assoc. Year Book*, XIV (Oct., 1938), 3-13.

Most of the chimneys are still standing, and as they reflected the light of the full moon as we drove up might well become the title of "Phantom Hill." There are the ruins of from forty to fifty buildings, including an observatory and a magazine; the latter was built entirely of stone and was so little injured that Dr. Birch took it for a company storehouse. The stable is also a fine stone building, so that, altogether, Phantom Hill is the cheapest and best new station on the route. There is a fine well, eighty feet deep and twenty feet in diameter, which, when we passed, had seventeen feet of water in it. One of the houses whose walls are nearly perfect is used by the station men. Mr. Burlington and his wife we found here all alone, hundreds of miles from any settlement, bravely stopping at their post on Phantom Hill, fearless of the attacks of blood-thirsty Indians—as brave a man as ever settled on a frontier and a monument of shame to the cowardly soldiers who burned the post. The fort is now needed to protect the frontier, and should form one of a great chain of military stations along the overland mail route, which needs all the protection that government has promised.

The station is directly in the trail of the northern Comanches as they run down into Texas on their marauding expeditions. To leave this and other stations on the route so exposed is trifling with human life, and inviting an attack on the helpless defenders of the mail. As I have already said, there will be designing white men as well as Indians whose cupidity must be overawed by adequate military protection. Let but this be afforded, and I predict for the mail route a complete success, as well as a rapid settlement of the many fertile and desirable spots along the line.

We had expected to find a team of mules in readiness for us at Phantom Hill, but as they were not there we had to proceed with our already jaded animals until we could meet them on their way towards us. Our mules had brought us already thirty-four miles at a good pace, but we had to go fifteen miles further, or half way to Abercrombie Peak, before we met another team. The road was across a smooth plain studded with the everlasting mesquite timber.

The Abercrombie Range is about midway between the Brazos and Colorado rivers, running northwest and southeast, and at the peak are a series of bluffs rising from the plain to the height of nearly 2,000 feet. The peak itself has a curious summit, or cap, of bare rocks, with regular interstices, as if a work of solid masonry. It seemed as if the rain had washed away the soil, leaving the rocks in this manner. At a distance they much resembled the turrets and abutments of a lofty fortress. They could be seen for thirty or forty miles of our road along the plain, and they looked so near that one naturally became impatient to reach them. A distance which would appear to be but a mile or two would prove to be eight or ten, thus affording another similitude of these vast plains to the broad sea, in the deceptive appearance of distances. It was at first fairly aggravating to travel for hours in plain sight of an object, and yet appear to be no nearer than when you started; but I afterwards learned to get accustomed to it.

We stopped at the station called Abercrombie Pass,[68] to get breakfast, which consisted of the standard—coffee, tough beef, and butterless short cake, prepared by an old

[68] Bailey refers to this station as Mountain Pass.

Negro woman, who, if cleanliness is next to godliness, would stand but little chance of heaven. There is an old saying that "every man must eat his peck of dirt." I think I have had good measure with my peck on this trip, which has been roughing it with a vengeance.

Leaving Abercrombie Peak, our road led through a rugged pass in the mountains, and up rather a steep hill, which I supposed of course had an incline on the other side. But what was my surprise on reaching the top to find a broad plain stretching before us. The keeper of the next station,[69] as well as of that at Abercrombie Peak, was appropriately named Lambshead, for he had a drove of 300 sheep grazing, growing, and increasing without expense to him, while he was attending to other duties.

A few hours' ride brought us to Chadbourne, a military station on a bend of the little Colorado River, exactly on the thirty-second parallel of latitude, where we arrived on Thursday afternoon, the 23d of September, nearly twenty-four hours ahead of table time, having traversed 955 miles of our journey without accident and but little delay.[70]

The most direct course to El Paso would be from this point along the thirty-second parallel, but the much dreaded Llano Estacado, or Stalked [Staked] Plain, interposes its waterless barrenness, and our course must still be in a southwesterly direction to the head of the Concho River, a tributary of the little Colorado, and thence to the "Horsehead Crossing" of the Pecos River, taking us

[69] Valley Creek.

[70] Fort Chadbourne was established Oct. 28, 1852, and abandoned as a military station in Dec., 1867. It was located on Oak Creek, 30 miles above its junction with the Colorado River. See Hamersly, Pt. II, p. 127.

a degree further south, which we have to regain by following up the Pecos—all of which might have been saved
had the money which has been expended in trying to sink
artesian wells on the Staked Plains [Plain] been applied to
the purpose of building plain tanks to catch the water
when it falls, as it often does in copious quantities. But I
had forgotten Chadbourne's. There is now but one company of the Second Cavalry stationed here—Company G—
the remaining cavalry and infantry having been ordered to
look after the Indians in the Wachita [Wichita] Mountains.[71]   There are few houses besides the government
buildings, and few inhabitants besides the soldiers. The
place is almost surrounded by a sort of barricade which
was built a few years since in anticipation of a sweeping
attack by the Indians—which did not come off. Some of
the buildings look unusually neat for this section of the
country. The officer now in command is Captain Bradfute,[72] who, I understand, kindly loaned the employees
of the mail company sufficient arms and ammunition for
their protection until their own could be forwarded.

Some little delay was experienced, here, before the wild
mules could be caught and harnessed, by which several
hours of our advance time was lost. Mr. J. B. Nichols
of Mr. Crocker's division was to drive, and Mr. Mather
of Mr. Glover's division, which commences at Chadbourne and ends at Franklin on the Rio Grande, was to
proceed on horseback, point out the road, and maintain

[71] Ormsby probably meant the Wichita Mountains in Indian Territory.
During the year 1858 there was considerable trouble between the Comanches of Texas and the Wichitas, necessitating military intervention. See
W. B. Morrison, *Military Posts and Camps in Oklahoma* (Oklahoma City,
1936), p. 100.

[72] William R. Bradfute, later a colonel in the Confederate army.

a general supervision. Whether from the inefficiency of
Mr. Nichols' driving, or because Mr. Mather's furious
riding frightened the mules, or because the mules were
wild, or that the boys had been having a jolly good time
on the occasion of the arrival of the first stage, or by a
special dispensation of Providence—or from a combination
of all these causes—I will not pretend to say, but certainly,
from some unforeseen and vexatious cause, we here suffered
a detention of some hours. The mules reared, pitched,
twisted, whirled, wheeled, ran, stood still, and cut up
all sorts of capers. The wagon performed so many evolu-
tions that I, in fear of my life, abandoned it and took to
my heels, fully confident that I could make more progress
in a straight line, with much less risk of breaking my
neck.

Mr. Lee, sutler at the fort, who, with others, had come
out on horseback to see us start, kindly offered to take
me up behind him—to which, though not much of an
equestrian, I acceded with the view of having a little better
sight of the sport at a safe distance. In this I was eminent-
ly gratified, for the gyrations continued to considerable
length, winding up with tangling all the mules pretty well
in the harness, the escape of one of the leaders into the
woods, and the complete demolition of the top of the
wagon; while those in charge of it lay around loose on
the grass, and all were pretty well tired out and disgusted,
except those who had nothing to do but look on.

For my part, I thought it the most ludicrous scene I
ever witnessed, though it seemed a great pity that time
which was needed on other parts of the route should be
thus wasted or lost here. Both of the leading mules having
escaped, and Mr. Mather having become completely anx-

ious that every one should go to the d——l, and understand
that he did not care a d——n for anyone, I thought the
progress of the mail, for that night at least, was stopped;
but Nichols averred that the mail should go on if he went
alone with the two wheel-mules; and, sure enough, he
started off after getting the harness once more disentan-
gled, and kept the road in fine style. I had fully made
up my mind by this time that it would be as much as my
life was worth to go under the existing circumstances, but,
seeing him go off, I rode up to him, and, finding persuasion
of no avail, overcame my strong objections and concluded
to go, though if I had had any property I certainly should
have made a hasty will. When I had become seated I
thought I would ascertain all the chances, and the following dialogue ensued between myself and Mr. Nichols:

"How far is it to the next station?"

"I believe it is thirty miles."

"Do you know the road?"

"No."

"How do you expect to get there?"

"There's only one road; we can't miss it."

"Have you any arms?"

"No, I don't want any; there's no danger."

Whether there was danger or not, I felt as if I had a
little rather have started under other circumstances; but I
was bound to go with the mail, though I had not much
confidence that our two mules could make the thirty
miles. Fortunately our course was a clear and straight
one, leading across an apparently boundless prairie, with
not a tree or shrub to be seen, the parched grass almost
glistening in the light of the moon.

The night was clear and bright, the road pretty level,

and the mules willing, and I soon ceased to regret having started. I alternately drove while Nichols slept, or slept while he drove, or rode horseback for the man who accompanied us to take back the team, and, altogether, passed a very pleasant night, though our progress was necessarily slow. But about 2 A.M. we came to a steep and stony hill, obstinately jutting from the prairie, right in our path and impossible of avoidance. One mule could neither be coaxed or driven up, so we had to camp until morning, when, after much difficulty, we ascended the hill and discovered the station fire, miles distant—a mere speck among the trees. We soon reached it and found it to be a corral, or yard, for the mules, and tents erected inside for the men, under charge of Mr. Henry Roylan. They had seen us coming and were herding the mules as we drove up. Their corral was built of upright rough timber, planted in the ground. They had pitched their tents inside, for fear of the Indians, and took turns standing guard, two hours on and two hours off.

The station was near Grape Creek,[73] a fine stream, and also near some fine timber—two desirable things not to be found everywhere in Texas. The distance from this point to the head of the Concho River being fifty-six miles, and there being no inhabited station between, we had to take, in addition to our own team of four mules, a *cavellado*,[74] or drove, of as many more, for a change at intervals along the route. The change of teams was soon made, and, Mr. Roylan taking the reins, we were off once more at a good pace. Our road lay over the rolling

[73] Grape Creek station.

[74] Probably *cavellado* is intended to be *cavallada* or *caballada;* however, Ormsby's spelling is retained.

prairies studded with mesquite timber. A few miles from Grape Creek we crossed the Concho, and then, leaving the old road, which follows its winding course, we took a new road, across the country, which has been made under the supervision of the company—a ride of about thirty miles, the new road being very passable. We strike the Concho again at a station[75] about twenty-five miles from Grape Creek and fifty-five miles from Chadbourne, after following the Concho to its source on the borders of the dreaded Staked Plain, where we arrived about 2:30 A.M. of [on] Saturday, the 25th of September.

We may now be said to have commenced the difficulties of the journey through the great plains or waterless deserts of Texas and mountains of New Mexico and California; while the grandest spectacles of our journey are yet to be seen and described, with the assurance that we are safely at Tucson, Arizona, just beyond the Pinaleno Mountains. I must leave the description of our interesting journey thither for my next letter.

[75] Unnamed.

Overland to California

Special Correspondence of the New York Herald
San Francisco, Oct. 10, 1858

Arrival of the First Overland Mail from St. Louis at San Francisco. Time—Twenty-three Days and Twenty-three Hours and a Half. The Rate of Speed on the Various Divisions. Continued Description of the Route. The Great Deserts. The Valleys of Rio Grande and Messilla [Mesilla], and the Gadsden Purchase. Proposed Celebration in San Francisco. Three Days Later News, &c., &c., &c.

SAFE and sound from all the threatened dangers of Indians, tropic suns, rattlesnakes, grizzly bears, stubborn mules, mustang horses, jerked beef, terrific mountain passes, fording rivers, and all the concomitants which envy, pedantry, and ignorance had predicted for all passengers by the overland mail route over which I have just passed, here am I in San Francisco, having made the passage from the St. Louis post office to the San Francisco post office in twenty-three days, twenty-three hours and a half, just one day and half an hour less than the time required by the Overland Mail Company's contract with the Post Office Department. The journey has been by no means as fatiguing to me as might be expected by a continuous ride of such duration, for I feel almost fresh enough to undertake it again.

The route is prolific in interest to the naturalist, the mineralogist, and all who love to contemplate nature in her wildest varieties, and throughout the whole 2,700 miles the interest in new objects is not allowed to flag. I have found the deserts teeming with curious plants and animal life, the mountain passes prolific in the grandest scenery, and the fruitful valleys suggestive of an earthly paradise; while, if this trip may be considered a criterion, the alleged danger from Indians is all a bugbear.

I have already given you from time to time the date of our departure from most of the stations, as compared with the date required by the time table of the company. Since my last, I have discovered that the time table was accidentally made out so as to require the trip to be made in twenty-four days and half an hour, or twenty-three hours and a half less than the contract time with the Post Office Department. Taking this into consideration, the following table of our time from St. Louis to San Francisco must be considered a record of a wonderful performance, in view of the fact that no allowance is made for changing horses or other detentions, and that this is the first through trip.

Those places mentioned in the time table, but which for various reasons the company did not touch, are left out. Your readers will recollect that the contract of the Overland Mail Company was for twenty-five days, and that although partly confined to a specified route they were at liberty to change such portions as should to them seem likely to impede the safe and speedy transmission of the mail if adhered to. They therefore availed themselves of the liberty in several instances. First, instead of crossing the Pecos River in Texas at the Emigrant Crossing between Toyah Creek and Horsehead Crossing and following up the Pecos on its western bank, they made their first trip up the Pecos on the eastern bank and crossed at a few miles above Pope's Camp, near the Delaware Creek, nearly on the thirty-second parallel—a distance of about one hundred and fifty miles. Second, instead of crossing the great California (or Colorado) Desert from Fort Yuma, California, to San Bernardino, they took a more southerly course, over thirty miles further, to obtain a more desirable supply of water, and omitting San Bernardino altogether. In making out the table, I have calculated these additional distances. The whole distance from St. Louis to San Francisco by this circuitous route is thus made to be 2,866 miles, comprising probably some of the most difficult roads in existence. Here are the tables:

Time Table of First Overland Mail—St. Louis to San Francisco

Place	Table Time for Leaving		Actual Time of Leaving		Miles from St. Louis
St. Louis, Mo., and Memphis, Tenn.	Sep. 16,	8 A.M.	Sep. 16,	8 A.M.	
P. R. R. terminus	Sep. 16,	6 P.M.	Sep. 16,	6:15 P.M.	160
Springfield, Mo.	Sep. 18,	7:45 A.M.	Sep. 17,	4 P.M.	303
Fayetteville [Ark.]	Sep. 19,	10:15 A.M.	Sep. 18,	12 M.	403
Fort Smith, Ark.	Sep. 20,	3:30 A.M.	Sep. 19,	3:30 A.M.	468
Sherman, Texas	Sep. 22,	12:30 A.M.	Sep. 20,	4:40 P.M.	673
Fort Belknap, do.	Sep. 23,	9 A.M.	Sep. 22,	7 A.M.	819½
Ft. Chadbourne, do.	Sep. 24,	3:15 P.M.	Sep. 23,	7 P.M.	955
El Paso	Sep. 28,	11 A.M.	Sep. 30,	5.50 A.M.	1,369
Soldier's Farewell	Sep. 29,	8:30 P.M.	Oct. 1,	10:15 A.M.	1,519
Tucson, Arizona	Oct. 1,	1:30 P.M.	Oct. 2,	10 P.M.	1,703
Gila River, Ariz.	Oct. 2,	9 P.M.	Oct. 3,	10 P.M.	1,844
Fort Yuma, Cal.	Oct. 4,	3 A.M.	Oct. 5,	6:15 A.M.	1,979
Ft. Tejon via Los Angeles	Oct. 7,	7:30 A.M.	Oct. 8,	4:33 A.M.	2,494
Visalia, Cal.	Oct. 8,	11:30 A.M.	Oct. 8,	11:50 P.M.	2,621
Fireburg [Firebaugh's] Ferry	Oct. 9,	5:30 A.M.	Oct. 9,	11:50 A.M.	2,703
Arr. San Fran.	Oct. 10,	8:30 A.M.	Oct. 10,	7:30 A.M.	2,866

Thus you will perceive that we arrived here an hour before the time table time, which, being twenty-three hours and a half less than contract time, made our passage twenty-three days, twenty-three hours and a half, and, deducting the difference of time between St. Louis and San Francisco, our passage was made in twenty-three days and twenty-three hours and a half—a feat never yet equalled in overland travel, since, including detentions and stoppages, changing horses, meals, &c., our average speed was a fraction over five miles an hour. It may seem slow at first, but, when the quality of road as shown in my details is considered, I think all will concede that it is remarkably quick time.

The following table shows very nearly the rate of speed of the stages over each division of the road, throwing off small fractions:

Rate of Speed from Point to Point

Miles per hour

Pacific Railroad terminus to Fort Smith, Ark._____5½
Fort Smith, Ark., to Sherman, Tex._____5½
Sherman, Tex., to Fort Chadbourne, Tex._____3¾
Fort Chadbourne, Tex., to Franklin, Tex.,
    opposite El Paso_____2⅔
El Paso to Tucson, Arizona_____9
Tucson, Arizona, to Los Angeles, Cal._____5
Los Angeles, Cal., to San Francisco, Cal._____9

The details which I have already given you of our journey to the head of the Concho River explained fully the nature of the roads up to that point. The low rate of speed between Chadbourne and El Paso is accounted for by the fact that that route comprises an entirely wild country across the great Staked Plain, seventy-five miles without water, and one hundred and thirteen miles up the sierras, where stations had not yet been established. In fact, there is not a human habitation, except the company stations, on this whole distance of over four hundred miles. Fortunately, the energy of Mr. Kinyon and his assistants on this end of the route made up the lost time of the others, and brought the mail in with flying colors. You will perceive by the table that from Franklin, opposite El Paso, the fastest time on the road was made.

My last letter containing any details of our trip left us at the head of the Concho River, a tributary of the little Colorado in Texas, just on the border of the great Plain Ertacade [Estacado], or Staked Plain, one of the savannas of America. It derives its name from a tradition that many years ago the Spaniards had a road staked upon it from San Antonio, Texas, to Santa Fé in New Mexico. It extends from the 30th to the 35th parallel, being one hundred and seventy-five miles wide at its greatest width, and entirely destitute of wood and water. Its northern boundary is an abrupt precipice nearly six hundred feet high, while on the south it is intersected by a range of barren sand hills rising seventy feet above the general level of the plain. These sand hills are of a very drifting nature, and often cover up the road.

It will not, then, be a matter of wonder that to the emigrant this fearful journey is fraught with many terrors. He sees in his imagination his cattle, and perhaps himself, suffering all the inexpressible pangs of thirst-pains, more unendurable than flaming fire or bleeding wounds. We have read of the anguish of the monarch of Phrygia, whom the gods doomed to unceasing confinement in the sight of sweet waters, which were never allowed to touch his lips; of the terrible tortures of the bold mariners in the Arctic seas; of the sailor with "Water, water, everywhere, and not a drop to drink"; of the fearful tortures of the tropics, and of the trains on the great desert of Sahara—but none can realize the pangs of that terrible gnawing without that sad experience which is almost always death. It was, then, with no little fear that I approached this, what I deemed the most dangerous part of the journey, where for a distance of seventy-five miles—the width of the plain at our crossing place—not a drop of water could be procured for all the wealth of the world. Indeed, I was so carried away with the horrors of the trip that it was some time before it occurred to me that we might carry some water in the wagons—which reflection finally consoled me not a little.

We reached the head of the Concha [Concho] River early on the morning of Saturday, the 25th of September, and found there a most comfortable camp.[76] The men had not yet had time to build a house and were living in tents. They had made a large corral of bushes and had a large stock of mules, which had been left them, before our arrival, by Mr. Glover, the superintendent of the line from Chadbourne to El Paso, who had gone on before us some hours. Our arrival was unexpected, and all haste was immediately made to get us something to eat and start us again on our journey. The good natured Dutchman who officiated as cook quickly ranged the tin cups and plates and got us some broiled bacon, shortcake, and coffee, which was considered quite an aristocratic meal for so early a settlement, and which our long ride certainly made acceptable, however different from New York fare.

[76] Bailey refers to this camp only as "Head of Concho."

At least an hour was lost in catching and harnessing wild mules for our team, and for the *cavellado*, or drove, which we were to take with us, having no other change of team for seventy-five miles. The frightened animals ran in terror round the corral, the greasy Mexicans wielded their larriettos [*las reatas*] and frightened them still more, so that by the time a mule was caught and harnessed, often nearly choked to death, he was almost always nearly tired out before his work had commenced. We got a team at last, however, and soon were on our way (with our wagon well supplied with canteens of water) to the great Staked Plain. After passing over a well weeded plain, we came to the Mustang Springs,[77] which are lodgements of water durable during most of the year. It was the last water before the seventy-five miles of desert, and we let our mules drink their fill. It was just after sunrise that we entered the desert road, and I was agreeably surprised to see, instead of a tedious sea of parched sand, a variety of curious though weird vegetation, while the whole plain was studded with mesquite bushes looking fresh enough, certainly. Our start was rather unfavorable, for before we left Mustang Springs two of our mules in the cavalcade made a stampede for home, and the other two soon followed suit, the latter only being recovered after a hard chase and a detention of another hour.

But the road was hard and smooth, and we were enabled to travel at a pretty fair gait when we got started. Indeed,

[77] The springs formed several lakes, or large pools, which were highly saline and were, in all, about three miles in length. See J. H. Byrne, "Diary of the Expedition," Appendix, John Pope's "Report of Exploration . . .", in *Report of the Secretary of War, Communicating the Several Pacific Railroad Explorations* . . . (Washington, 1855), II, [pt. 4,] 93; also in *Reports of Explorations and Surveys* . . . (Washington, 1855-61), II (pt. 4, App. A), 71-72.

the road was literally baked hard in the scorching sun. The vast quantity of mesquite bushes somewhat surprised me. The leaves much resemble the cedar, but the stalk on the plain seldom grows thicker than a gooseberry bush. Many of the bushes were covered with ripe beans, resembling our string beans in appearance. They are excellent feed for stock, and it is said the Indians make a sort of meal of them.

There was an abundance of large cactus plants of numberless varieties, chittim [chittam] wood, and soap weed —the roots of which are used by the Indians for soap— and several kinds of grass. There are many places where it is evident that water has stood for some time since the last rain. One of the most curious plants was what is called the Spanish dagger, which grows in many varieties on this plain. The leaves are long, and tapered to a sharp point, and being very tough may well be called daggers. They are very sharp and tough, and I have been told that an antelope has been shot that had one of these leaves run clear through his foreleg. The plant grows often in large bunches like sheaves of grain and may easily be mistaken for them. In the twilight they may easily be transformed into imaginary Indians by the timid. The leaves may be made to appear as the tuft of his head or his outstretched arms, while its thickness is quite the consistency of an ordinary Indian. I often mistook them for men as we passed along.

As we travelled leisurely through the desert, we were refreshed with a decidedly cool and delicious breeze, while the atmosphere was by no means so unpleasant to me as in New York in a hot August day, though we were then about half way between the thirtieth and thirty-second parallels of latitude. There seemed to be an abundance of animal life on the desert. We saw large droves of antelopes frequently, and numbers of quail, snipe, and other specimens of the feathered tribe, while the "dog towns," or holes, of the prairie dogs were innumerable. This animal seems to be a cross between a squirrel and a rat terrier, and lives in holes which it digs in the ground. As we approached their towns we could see their shaking tails as they rushed frightened to their homes. They live on grass and weeds, and never trouble anybody except by undermining the road with their subterranean borings.

With all these evidences of animal and vegetable life, and the delightful breeze, I could not realize that I was in a desert. It seemed impossible that so much life could exist without a constant, never failing supply of water. But there were the evidences strewn along the road, and far as the eye could reach along the plain—decayed and decaying animals, the bones of cattle and sometimes of men (the hide drying on the skin in the arid atmosphere), all told a fearful story of anguish and terrific death from the pangs of thirst. For miles and miles these bones strew the plain—the silent witnesses of the eternal laws of nature, which, in the hope of gain, man hesitates not to brave. They are silent but speaking monuments of undeviating fate.

As we proceeded the plain grew more dreary and the vegetation less thick, until finally it relapses into a dull plain with scattered grass spots and stunted mesquite trees. In the morning the monotony of our ride was varied by the sight of a huge rattlesnake, which was promptly despatched by our driver named Jones, of Herculean frame, from which he has been surnamed the "baby." He daringly poked out a stick for the reptile to bite, and then coolly twisted off the rattle on his tail—which he gave to me.

In the afternoon we got up quite an excitement over a cloud of dust which was at first taken to be Mr. Glover and his train. The mules were whipped up, the horns blown, and a general excitement raised among the four in the wagon. Much to our chagrin, on finding ourselves disappointed, we were obliged to stop frequently and allow our jaded mules to rest and graze, though we had no water for them. It struck me that if one of the men had been left, and his weight of water brought in his place, we should have been somewhat better off. The plain is somewhat rolling, yet we found much difficulty in urging our mules down hill; and, notwithstanding my first favorable impression, I soon pronounced the great Staked Plain a bore. We were nearly twenty-four hours in crossing; and what seemed to me most remarkable was the extreme cold of the night after the warmth of the day. I found that my two blankets were by no means too warm.

As I lay dozing on the seat, about three o'clock on Sunday morning, I heard a cry from Jones that we had reached the Pecos River, and there we were, true enough, right into it. After hallooing and blowing our horn, we obtained an answer, as we supposed, from the other side of the river, telling us to drive up stream, which advice we followed, when to our astonishment we found ourselves in camp on the same side of the river.[78] The fact is, the Pecos makes such a turn here that you can hardly tell which side you are on. It is a swift stream, with a good body of water, rising away up in the Rocky Mountains

[78] Horsehead Crossing.

and emptying into the Rio Grande. It is much the color of the Mississippi. There were no trees nor any unusual luxuriance of foliage on the banks at the point where we struck it; so that if our driver had not been on the lookout we might have been wallowing in its muddy depth.

We found that Mr. Glover had arrived with his train but a few hours before us and had brought the stock for stocking the road. He had employed, here, fifteen Mexicans, or "greasers" as they are more commonly called—and a more miserable looking set of fellows I never saw. They stood shivering over the fire, and had to be fairly driven off to get the things in readiness for our immediate departure; and then ensued another hallooing and lassoing time with the wild mules, occupying more precious time and much patience, besides trying the animals' strength beyond endurance; but we got started at 4:30 A.M. on Sunday, the 26th, for a pretty long ride up the east, or northeast, bank of the Pecos.

The person in charge of the mail from this point was Captain Skillman, an old frontier man who was the first to run the San Antonio and Santa Fé mail at a time when a fight with the Indians, every trip, was considered in the contract. He is a man about forty-five years of age, in appearance much resembling the portraits of the Wandering Jew, with the exception that he carries several revolvers and bowie knives, dresses in buckskin, and has a sandy head of hair and beard. He loves hard work and adventures, and hates "Injuns," and knows the country about here pretty well.[79]

[79] Capt. Henry Skillman was awarded the first contract, in 1850, for transporting mail between San Antonio and El Paso. He distinguished himself by his bravery while a volunteer member of the Doniphan expedition, and later served gallantly in the southern army. See Owen White, *Out of*

We started with four mules to the wagon and eighteen in the *cavellado;* but the latter dwindled down in number as one by one the animals gave out. Most of them had but just been brought across the Staked Plain on the previous day and were pretty well tired out before they started. The prospect seemed pretty dreary for us at the outset, as we had 113 miles to travel before we could get any fresh stock, and those in the *cavellado* were our only hope for a change during the whole distance. But no others could be had and we were obliged to do with them and make the best time we could, which turned out to be bad enough.

Our course lay up the Pecos on what is called Pope's new road, having been made by Captain Pope's artesian well expedition in 1857. It was full of stumps and bunches of weeds which made it by no means pleasant riding in the thorough braced wagons, for the jolting was almost interminable and insufferable, and I frequently wished that Captain Pope could experience my ride over his road. After riding sixteen miles we met a train of wagons belonging to Mr. McHenry, who was going from San Francisco to San Antonio, carrying a load of grain for the company on the way. By his invitation we stopped and breakfasted with him, giving our mules a chance to eat,

---

the Desert: *The Historical Romance of El Paso* [El Paso, 1923], pp. 36, 65. R. E. Twitchell (*The Leading Facts of New Mexican History* [Cedar Rapids, Ia., 1912], II, 390) says that Capt. Skillman was killed "at Spencer's Ranch, near Presidio del Norte, April 15, 1864, while attempting to carry the Confederate mail into Texas."

J. M. Farwell, special correspondent of the *Alta California*, who left for St. Louis on the overland stage in October, 1858, and sent his paper a series of letters covering the trip, notes that Skillman's station was twenty-five miles from Pope's Camp. This Skillman may have been the one described by Ormsby. (*Weekly Alta California*, Nov. 27, 1858.)

drink, and rest—all of which they much needed. On hitching up we had another exhibition of the efficiency of the wild mule system, losing another half hour for the amusement of the Mexicans, who dexterously larrietted the animals, threw and harnessed them, and considered it wano [*bueno*] (good).

We finally got under way again and pursued our weary course along the edge of the plain, thumping and bumping at a rate which threatened not to leave a whole bone in my body. What with the dust and the sun pouring direct-ly on our heads—we leaving the wagon which was so unceremoniously uncovered at Chadbourne—I found that day's ride quite unpleasant, and at our several camps read-ily availed myself of the opportunity to plunge into the Pecos, muddy as it was; and I was heartily glad when about 10 P.M. we reached a station fifty-eight miles from our starting point of the morning—that was Horsehead Cross-ing of the Pecos.

This was a few miles above Emigrant Crossing, and our course still lay up the river, as it had been deemed advis-able to change the route in this respect. We found no mules at the station and left a few of ours.[80] The three Americans in charge of the station had, with the assistance of half a dozen "greasers," built a very fine "adobe" corral, and had started a house of the same material, and calculated that they could defend the stock against a whole tribe of Indians. This seemed to be the only fear at any of these stations—that the Indians would steal the stock. They never fight for glory, and seldom care about fight-ing openly, even for the purpose of stealing. They had not yet troubled this camp, though several had been seen

[80] Emigrant Crossing station.

in the vicinity. They were principally of the Apache tribe, a very numerous and troublesome body in this section of the country.

We continued our weary and dusty road up the Pecos on Monday, the 27th, inhaling constant clouds of dust and jolting along almost at snail's pace. Our animals kept giving out so that we had to leave them on the road; and by the time we reached Pope's Camp at least half a dozen had been disposed of in this way. As we neared Pope's Camp, in the bright moonlight, we could see the Guadalupe Mountains, sixty miles distant on the other side of the river, standing out in bold relief against the clear sky, like the walls of some ancient fortress covered with towers and embattlements. I am told that on a clear day this peak has been seen across the plains for the distance of over one hundred miles, so tall is it and so low the country about it.

Pope's Camp is situated near the river, and was the locality from whence he proceeded to make his expensive experiments in boring artesian wells for two successive years.[81] I believe the appropriations to defray the expenses of these fruitless efforts to obtain water in the Staked Plain were first $100,000, and afterwards $60,000, all of which has been expended with the exception of about $15,000 of the last appropriation. Besides this, there were the expenses of two companies of dragoons and a large

[81] Capt. Pope first drilled near Delaware Creek, in the spring of 1855. He continued in charge of the artesian wells experiment until 1859, at which time the project was abandoned. See *Message from the President . . . To . . . Congress . . . First Session . . . Thirty-fourth Congress*, Pt. II (34th Cong., 1st Sess., Senate *Ex. Doc.*, No. 1; Washington, 1855), pp. 94-98; *Reports of Explorations and Surveys . . .,* VII, "Conclusion," pp. 16-18, 31-33; *Appendix to the Congressional Globe* (Washington, 1858), 34th Cong., 3d Sess., p. 26; *ibid.*, 35th Cong., 1st Sess., p. 35; *ibid.*, 36th Cong., 1st Sess., p. 12.

quartermaster's department. Capt. Pope bored one well to the depth of 1,140 feet, but eventually reported that the scheme would require more expensive machinery; and so the project of procuring water on the Staked Plains [Plain] was for a time abandoned, and the buildings of Pope's Camp are now used by the Overland Mail Company as a station. They are built of adobe in a substantial manner, and form quite a little town.

We stopped just long enough to get some supper of shortcake, coffee, dried beef, and raw onions, and taking a fresh team started on a sixty mile journey to the Guadalupe mountain. With a single team of four mules we forded the Pecos about three miles above Pope's Camp, the stream being quite rapid and nearly covering the hubs of our wagon. Our course lay along the same prairie country as on the other side of the river; and after running about thirty miles we camped at sunrise near the head of the Delaware Creek,[82] cooked our breakfast with a fire of buffalo "chips"—a fuel which makes excellent manure —and expected to have a nice cup of coffee, when upon examining our pack we found that it had been overlooked in the hurry, and we had to content ourselves with jerked beef (cooked on the "chips"), raw onions, crackers slightly wormy, and a bit of bacon. The stomach, however, does not long remain delicate after a few days of life on the plains, and our breakfast was quite acceptable to me, notwithstanding the buffalo "chips," which struck me as rather a novel and at first distasteful idea.

The Guadalupe Peak loomed up before us all day in the most aggravating manner. It fairly seemed to be further

[82] Bailey records a station at Delaware Springs, forty miles from Pope's Camp.

off the more we travelled, so that I almost gave up in despair all hopes of reaching it. Our last eight or ten miles were among the foothills of the range, and I now confidently believed we were within a mile or two, at the outside. But the road wound and crooked over the interminable hills for miles yet and we seemed to be no nearer than before. I could see the outlines of the mountain plainly, and, as I eagerly asked how far it was, the captain laughingly told me it was just five miles yet, and we had better stop and give the animals a little rest or they never could finish it. I should not have had the slightest hesitance in attempting to walk the distance in a few minutes, so near did it seem.

We camped at Independence Spring—about five miles from the peak—a natural curiosity, in its way, for the sand boils up constantly a few feet from the surface, while the depth of the spring is said to be fifteen feet. The water was exceedingly cool, and is believed to be the same that bubbles up near the mouth of the Delaware below, and the piney woods above, sinking in the ground and rising again twice.

We were obliged actually to beat our mules with rocks to make them go the remaining five miles to the station, which is called the Pinery on account of the number of pine trees that grow in the gorge of the mountain in which it is situated. As we approached the mountain, the hills and gulleys bore the appearance of having been created by some vast, fierce torrent rushing around the base of the peak, and tearing its way through the loose earth. The comparative scarcity of stone all over the Staked Plain and up to the very foot of the mountain is also noticeable, and it seems as if nature had saved all her ruggedness to pile it up in this colossal form of the Guadalupe Peak, which rears its head four thousand feet above the level of the plain, and seven thousand above the level of the sea. This great height of the plains above the level of the sea will account in some measure for the deliciously cool breezes of which I have spoken.

We found the corral built of heavy pine timber—a very scarce article, indeed, except on the mountains—and after getting another stereotype meal, with the addition of some venison pie and baked beans, we started with a fresh team for a sixty mile ride to the Carnudas [Cornudos] mountain, through the Guadalupe Cañon. The wild grandeur of the scene in the cañon is beyond description. The peak itself, sometimes called Cathedral Peak, towers full 600 feet above the base of the cañon, where is the tortuous, white, sandy bed of a stream which was now dry but which in the rainy season must be a fierce torrent.

The road winds over some of the steepest and stoniest hills I had yet seen, studded with inextricable rocks, each one of which seems ready to jolt the wagon into the abyss below. It is enough to make one shudder to look at the perpendicular side of the cañon and think what havoc one mischievous man could make with an emigrant train passing through the cañon.

The great peak towers as if ready any moment to fall, while huge boulders hang as if ready, with the weight of a rain drop, to be loosened from their fastenings and descend with lumbering swiftness to the bottom, carrying destruction in their paths. The water appears to have washed away the soil of the peak and its minor hills, revealing the strata like so many regularly built walls of a fortress, and the whole mass presents a scene of stupendous grandeur. Just before the bottom of the cañon is reached there stands by the roadside the grave of a Mexican guide, who had ventured in advance of his party and was murdered by the Indians[83]—a thrilling reminder of another of the dangers of this dreadful pass.

We got through about sunset, and I never shall forget the gorgeous appearance of the clouds: tinged by the setting sun above those jagged peaks, changing like a rapid panorama, they assumed all sorts of fantastic shapes, from frantic maidens with dishevelled hair to huge monsters of fierce demeanor, chasing one another through the realms of space. We had hardly passed through before the sound of voices and the gleaming of a light denoted that there was a party ahead of us. The awe inspiring scenery and the impressive sunset had almost set me dreaming as I lay listlessly in the wagon; but the possibility of meeting foes, perhaps a band of murderous Indians, in this wild and lonely spot filled me for a time with fears; but I had great faith in the captain's prowess, and felt somewhat easier when he declared it to be his opinion that the party was an American one.

In a moment we were upon them, and, to our astonishment, found that it was the overland mail which left San Francisco on the 15th [of] September, with five through passengers, and which was now eight hours ahead of time. After exchanging congratulations and telling bits of news, both parties passed on, I availing myself of the opportunity

[83] J. M. Farwell reported that the guide was "in Capt. Longstreet's company, 8th infantry. He was sent forward to look for water, and when in the narrowest portion of the pass, he was shot full of arrows by some Apache Indians. There is set up at his head a stone upon which is inscribed 'Jose Maria Palancio, Guide, killed Feb. 1st, 1855, by Indians.'" See *Weekly Alta California*, Nov. 27, 1858.

to send to the *Herald* a despatch which I had nearly written for the occasion.

We camped at Crow Spring, within about thirty miles of the Carnudas [Cornudos] mountain. The spring is of sulphur but palatable enough when one is thirsty. It is situated on a level plain some distance from the road, and would be passed unnoticed were it not known to the traveller. The road from the Guadalupe to Carnudas [Cornudos] is a gradual ascent, with grass and mesquite bushes similar to the rest of the plain. The Guadalupe Mountains were plainly visible from all points of the route, as were also the Carnudas [Cornudos], which are separate peaks of jagged rocks jutting up from the plain to the height of about 1,500 feet. The rocks or boulders are of red sandstone, and on the principal peak are of an oblong character, set with such remarkable regularity as to appear to be the work of art. The water collects in natural basins from the rain and stands the year round. As yet they have furnished a sufficient supply of water, and if not adequate can easily be enlarged. There are four principal peaks, which appear to be ranged in a square. There is quite a large station here,[84] and we procured a fresh team and a side driver and set out for Waco [Hueco] Tanks, thirty-six miles distant.

About sixteen miles on the road we passed the Alamos Wells, which are springs in a mountain about half a mile from the road, though apparently but a few yards. From these wells to the Waco [Hueco] Tanks—a distance of twenty miles—there is no water. Within about six miles of the Waco [Hueco] Tanks is the Sierra [Cerro] Alto, a high mountain which can be seen almost immediately

[84] Cornudos de los Alamos.

after leaving the Carnudas [Cornudos]. The road all the way is excellent, being a rolling plain with the exception of a very steep hill near the Sierra [Cerro] Alto, down which I much feared we could not descend in safety; but our driver seemed to know every stone and we whirled along on the very brink of the precipices with perfect safety, though the night was quite dark.

On reaching the Waco [Hueco] Tanks[85] we found an excellent corral and cabin built; but to our consternation the station keeper pointed to two eight gallon kegs, saying, "that is all the water we have left for a dozen men and as many head of cattle." The Waco [Hueco] Tanks have been reported to be inexhaustible, but the unusual droughts had drained them, and the most rigorous search through the mountain did not bring to light any more. The tank had been recently enlarged so as to hold water enough to last a year when the rain next fell, but until that time the station would have to be abandoned unless by chance water could be found in the vicinity. We changed horses here and took supper, and a few hours' ride brought us to Franklin city on the Rio Grande river, opposite the ancient town of El Paso.

As we neared the river the delightful aroma of the fruit and herbs was most grateful after so long and dreary a ride over the desert, and at that moment I could have endorsed all the encomiums on "the fertile valley of the Rio Grande." We passed many vineyards and comfortable ranches built of adobe and looking extremely neat. About two miles from Franklin is Fort Bliss,[86] now occupied by

[85] Natural cisterns.

[86] Established Feb. 11, 1848. See Hamersly, *Complete Regular Army Register*, Pt. II, p. 125. According to C. C. Rister (*The Southwestern*

a small garrison of United States troops. The fort is built of adobe.

The city of Franklin,[87] on the American side of the river, contains a few hundred inhabitants, and is in the midst of a fine agricultural district. The onions as well as the grapes of this locality are of world-wide celebrity, and El Paso wines are universally appreciated. As we arrived very early in the morning and did not cross the river, I had not even a chance of seeing El Paso.[88] Here, Mr. Glover's division ends, and in justice to him, as well as in explanation of the very slow time which we made over his route—a little less than three miles per hour, including detentions—I must say that he has active preparations on foot for increasing his stations and improving the character of his stock, both of which are very desirable.

We left Franklin at 5:40 A.M. on Thursday, the 30th, for Messilla [Mesilla], our route leading through the valley of the Rio Grande and the Messilla [Mesilla], which are always known as "fertile." To my great relief the mules were dispensed with for a while and a good team of California horses substituted, which spun the wagon over the ground at a rate which was quite new to me. Our road led over a part of that for the improvement of which, between Franklin and Fort Yuma, Col. Leach obtained a pretty fat appropriation from Congress. I feel

Frontier, 1865-1881 [Cleveland, 1928], p. 62) it was first designated "Post El Paso," and later, Mar. 8, 1854, named Fort Bliss.

[87] Named by Benjamin Franklin Coontz when he was appointed the first postmaster in 1852. The name was changed to El Paso in 1859. See White, Out of the Desert, p. 43.

[88] El Paso, or El Paso del Norte, Mexico, is now known as Ciudad Juárez.

convinced that the road must have been a terrible one, indeed, if he could have improved it any, for I then believed his portion to be about the steepest and stoniest I had seen. The company use but a few miles of it, in going from Franklin to Yuma, preferring to travel the old route. The road after leaving Franklin is quite hilly and dusty, though tolerably good.

About twenty-one miles from Franklin we changed horses at a station in a pretty grove of cottonwood trees[89]—the only habitation before reaching Fort Fillmore, eighteen miles further on. This fort consists of half a dozen adobe buildings. There are now but seventy-five men stationed there, under command of Lieutenant Friedly [Freedley],[90] and they are under orders to leave for Fort Defiance, where the Indians are very troublesome.[91]

Six miles further on we came to Messilla [Mesilla]— but not the Messilla [Mesilla] which I had pictured in my imagination as the thrifty town of a fertile valley. True, the fields were groaning with the weight of heavy crops, the dykes or irrigating canals were abundant, and the soil had every appearance of being capable of producing anything that the wants of man might desire or his labors bring forth; but the people, mostly Mexicans, were squalid

[89] Designated "Cottonwoods" by Bailey.

[90] Lieut. Henry W. Freedley (1832-89). See G. W. Cullum, *Biographical Register of the Officers and Graduates of the U. S. Military Academy* (3d ed.; Boston, 1891), II, 635-36.
Fort Fillmore was established Sept. 23, 1851, and abandoned July 26, 1861. See Hamersly, Pt. II, p. 133; M. L. Crimmins, "Fort Fillmore," *New Mex. Hist. Rev.,* VI, 327-33.

[91] Fort Defiance was located about 190 miles west of the present Albuquerque. For an account of the Indian troubles see F. D. Reeve, "The Federal Indian Policy in New Mexico, 1858-1880," *New Mex. Hist Rev.,* XII, 223-47; Twitchell, *Leading Facts of New Mexican History,* II, 315-20.

and dirty—their houses were built of adobe and sticks, looking more like miserable dog kennels than human habitations on the outskirts of a city. The people seemed to luxuriate in filth, and basked in the sun with all the complacency of overfed animals. How different, I thought, would be this valley were it peopled by a few of our steady eastern farmers; I could not but conclude that Providence knew just the right place to put the lazy men to keep them lazy, and the industrious ones to keep them industrious. Here is a vast valley whose soil will yield but for the planting two crops per year, and yet it does not bring forth a tithe of its productiveness, because its people are lazy and indolent, and prefer to live in mud houses and bask in the sunshine, when, by a little labor, they might live in palaces with eastern magnificence.

In Messilla [Mesilla] city the houses are little better than on the outskirts. There are about three thousand inhabitants, and I never saw such a miserable set of people in my life. A few speculating Yankees live here and are making fortunes rapidly by their enterprise in keeping stores. They get what prices they please for what goods they please. Lumber is $200 per thousand feet, and everything else in proportion except grain and hay, which are comparatively cheap. But the people are obnoxious to the view, and I was as glad to get out of Messilla [Mesilla] as I had been anxious to get into it.[92] Between Fort Fillmore and Messilla [Mesilla] we forded the Rio Grande

[92] Mesilla was established by a colony of New Mexicans who did not wish to become American citizens, following the treaty of Guadalupe Hidalgo in 1848. The town, however, was included in the Gadsden Purchase. For further information about the town and the valley see George Griggs, *History of Mesilla Valley; or, The Gadsden Purchase* (Mesilla, 1930); P. M. Baldwin, "A Short History of the Mesilla Valley," *New Mex. Hist. Rev.*, XIII, 314-24.

—at this point but an insignificant puddle, being very low. The water is very muddy and the shifting quicksands change the bed of the river much. Indeed, a few miles below El Paso the river has taken a new channel and added several towns to the American territory.

The Messilla [Mesilla] Valley is a vast plain, encircled by mountains and presenting an appearance very similar to the hundred other valleys of New Mexico and California, which seem like vast amphi-theatres and present considerable sameness, with the exception of their susceptibility to cultivation. The principal peak in sight is Stevenson's [or Stephenson's] silver mine,[93] which is, I believe, being worked to considerable advantage. A few miles from Messilla [Mesilla][94] we changed our horses for another team of those interminable mules, and started on a dreary ride of fifty-two miles for Cooke's Spring. This is the commencement of that series of deserts without water extending from the Rio Grande to the Gila—one of the most tedious portions of the route.

Our road lay through what was called the Pecatch [Picacho] Pass, and, as I walked nearly all the way through it, it seemed to me rather mountainous. It was about two miles long and had some very bad hills. In comparison with other passes and cañons on the route, it was not very bad, though quite bad enough and all up hill. When, however, we reached the summit, we were upon the border of a broad and level plain extending as

[93] According to P. M. Baldwin (*ibid.*, pp. 315-16), Don Antonio García, of El Paso, first worked the mine about 1819, but trouble with the Apaches forced him to abandon it. "In later times the García grant was purchased by Hugh Stephenson, of El Paso, and the mine was reopened. It is now known as the Bennett-Stephenson mine."

[94] Picacho, opposite Doña Ana.

far away as the eye could reach. At our backs were the ranges of the Oregon [Organ] Mountains, the debris of the Rocky Mountains, forming the eastern boundary of the Messilla [Mesilla] Valley. In front we could just see in the distance Cooke's Peak, rising from the plain in bold prominence from among the surrounding hills.

A few miles beyond Cooke's Spring, which we left shortly after 12:30 A.M., of Friday, the 1st inst., we met the second mail from San Francisco for St. Louis. A ride of about twenty miles brought us to Membrace [Mimbres] River,[95] a stream of not much consequence, and the road with few if any objects of interest beyond the ordinary plains which I have described. Seventeen miles further west are the Cow Springs [Spring][96] in the centre of the plain, and thirty-one miles from them the Soldier's Farewell Springs[97] of a similar nature, the water being good and durable. All this prairie land through which we pass, here, and which is now a barren, uninhabited waste, might with a little irrigation be made to produce almost anything.

Soldier's Farewell, like Cow Spring and Cooke's Spring, consists simply of one tent for the accommodation of the station men, whose fare is about like that which I have already described at other stations, and which I shared. We left Soldier's Farewell on the 1st inst., at 10:15 A.M., having to go forty-two miles to Stein's Peak without water, across a rolling plain with a smooth, hard road, part of which I must credit to Col. Leach. We had learned on our way that the station at Stein's Peak[98] was a favorite

95 Bailey notes a station at this point.
96 Bailey gives only the Spanish name, "Ojo de la Vaca."
97 Bailey also gives the Spanish name, "Los Penasquitos."
98 Bailey also gives the Spanish name, "El Peloncillo."

camping ground for the Apache Indians, and that but a few days before a band of two hundred and fifty, headed by Chief Mongas [Mangas],[99] had gone to the station and demanded the gift of twenty sacks of corn, telling the men they had "better hurry it up d——d quick." We met with no adventure on the road but a few shots at "Key-o-tahs" [coyotes], and seeing a couple of harmless Indians; but in view of what had happened it may be judged that we were a little anxious on approaching the station, for if, instead of the corral we should see a heap of smoking ruins and an Indian camp, we might not expect to pass without some difficulty.

The location of the station was in a little hollow under the mountain, so that we could not see it until we were within a few hundred yards of it. I can assure you that it was with no little relief that, as we ascended the last hill, we saw the corral still safe and the men moving about. But for a moment we were in doubt—we had come in full view of the place and had not yet seen a man, and several moments of the most anxious suspense ensued ere we were quite relieved. It was now growing dark on the night of the 1st instant, and the delightful moon which nearly all the way had cheered our midnight travel was now no more to be seen. We had to pass through the Apache, or "Doubtful," Pass—so called from the supposed great danger from the narrowness of the road and the frequency

[99] Mangas Coloradas (Red Sleeve), a Mimbreño Apache chief, caused considerable trouble in the Southwest. He was killed in 1863. See F. W. Hodge, *Handbook of American Indians* (4th impression; Washington, 1912), I, 799-800; Woodworth Clum, *Apache Agent* (Boston, 1936), *passim*; R. H. Ogle, "Federal Control of the Western Apaches, 1848-1886," *New Mex. Hist. Rev.*, XIV, 338-54, *passim*.

of Indians; we were, in fact, entering the most dangerous portion of the Apache country.

I swallowed a hasty supper—beef, bacon, and shortcake— for the purpose of getting through the pass as soon as possible. The pass could not be seen to advantage, though I could discern upon each side of the narrow road the perpendicular rocks, apparently ready to fall upon us. The distance to the next station was thirty-seven miles, and ten of these lay through this pass. I was not sorry when we got through, though we did not meet a soul, except, just as we started, the American consul at El Paso and a friend.

The next station was called Apache Pass,[100] and from thence we had another thirty-seven mile ride over more monotonous plains skirted with high hills, to Dragoon Springs, the scene of the awful attempted murder of three Americans by four Mexicans, at one of the company's stations. I have already given you the particulars of this affair in a former letter—giving the names of Burr and an old man named Cunningham, as the killed, and a young man named St. John, from New York, defending himself bravely with his pistol, and escaping. I believe he still lives, and has received a large number of letters which were sent him by the first overland mail. It would seem hard that he should die, after surviving the pains of hunger and thirst and bleeding wounds for four days and three nights.

From Dragoon Springs the appearance of the country for the next twenty-five miles is entirely different from the preceding. The road leads through deep gulleys and beds of creeks and over walls; and once more we came to

[100] Bailey also gives the Spanish name, "Puerto del Dado."

the interminable mesquite timber, looking like crab apple trees or stunted oak—when suddenly we wheeled into the valley of the San Pedro. The stream itself is insignificant, but the valley has the appearance of having been once a vast stream of itself—bordered, as it is, by the bluffs of an abruptly ending plain, far above its level, on the west, and sloping hills on the east. Our road led a few miles north in this valley—in which there is not, that we could see, a respectably sized tree—and finally crossed the stream[101] (if by that name it might be dignified) and took a westerly course over the hills, from which we had a fine view of the San Pedro Valley. However uninviting this valley may appear, it is said to be very fertile; but so long as it is left, as now, a prey to merciless Indians, no man can settle there in safety. If there is any portion of the route calculated to impress one with the necessity of military protection for the route of this overland mail, it is this very last few hundred miles which I have just described, running through the heart of the Apache country.

Our road now leads us to the Ciniqua [Cienega] River —the only evidence of which is its fine white sandy bed, through which we drag wearily for four miles. The land, however, is good, and capable of cultivation; at present it is covered for the whole length of the river with a species of coarse salt grass, which grows to a great height, and large numbers of sun flowers, which were quite welcome after the flowerless hills and deserts through which we had passed. On the banks of the valley are some of the largest cactus plants I had yet seen, towering to a height of from ten to twelve feet, and often even higher, with bodies of full two feet in diameter. We ascend from

101 Bailey lists a station at the San Pedro River.

the valleys of the Ciniqua [Cienega], with its beautiful grass and weeds, to the mountainous district approaching Tucson, the first city in Arizona, after leaving Messilla [Mesilla], worthy of any note. We change our horses before leaving the Ciniqua [Cienega],[102] for its heavy sand and the coming hard hills are very wearing upon the animals.

After some hard tugging we find ourselves up the last hill, and apparently on a mountain plain, while just peeping above its base we see on every side the tops of other mountains, jutting their craggy peaks against the sky in all their rugged grandeur. The sun is rapidly setting, and, while in the west we behold the declining day, in the east there are signs of fast falling night. The heavy clouds lower over the mountain tops, tinged with the rays of the sun, in all the colors of the rainbow, quickly changing their forms, even as we gaze on them, and resolving themselves into curious shapes resembling numberless animate and inanimate objects. The peaks of the western mountains, standing out in bold relief from the glaring rays of the sun immediately behind them, seem to be the tall spires and housetops of a burning city or the turrets of a fortress blazing with cannon, and we almost listen for the wail of the sufferer or the roar of artillery. Immediately around us the tall plants of the Spanish dagger appear like so many soldiers standing guard in the darkness of the night, till we almost expect them to cry, "Halt, and give the countersign."

It was while indulging in this dreamy reverie that I

[102] Bailey lists this as Seneca Springs, or "Cienega de los Pimas." Cienega was generally pronounced "Sinicky," or "Senicky," by the uninformed, according to W. C. Barnes in his *Arizona Place Names* ("University of Arizona Bulletin," VI, No. 1; Tucson, 1935), p. 96.

was aroused by the driver's unpoetic voice: "Halloa! Here's the western mail in a muss!" And, sure enough, it was the third mail from San Francisco, about twelve miles from Tucson, two days ahead of time, but in a decided muss from two balkey lead horses tangled in the harness. We lent our assistance, causing some delay, and finally lent our driver, who, to expedite them, agreed to drive back on his lonely road of seventy-five miles to Dragoon Springs, which he had just traversed with us. We proceeded on, reaching Tucson at 9:30 P.M. of Saturday, the 2d inst., and leaving there about 10 P.M.

I had expected to close the details of the journey with this letter, in time for the mail which leaves here at a little after twelve o'clock tonight, but find myself, at nearly the time of closing, only describing the route to a point within 1,163 miles of San Francisco, with some very interesting portions of it yet to describe, including the great California deserts and some of her fertile valleys. Arrangements are being made here, now, to have some kind of a public demonstration in honor of the success of the enterprise so unexpectedly flattering, and in my next I shall give you an account of that, as well as the concluding details of my journey and the description of the latter end of the route.

Our San Francisco Correspondence

San Francisco, Oct. 10, 1858

The Arrival of the First Overland Mail in San Francisco. Fraser River Mines, &c.

The arrival, this morning, of the first overland mail coach from St. Louis in less than twenty-four days has caused a general rejoicing throughout the city. Our citizens are determined to mark their appreciation of the importance of opening this route, and the era it inaugurates in the history of California. A meeting is called for tomorrow evening, when an expression of opinion will be made concerning the magnitude and prospective results of this great enterprise. It will be one of the largest ever held in San Francisco.[103] It is difficult at this moment to realize the full importance to the Pacific Coast of the establishment of overland mail routes. We will cease to be considered any longer a distant dependency—a colony, as it were. We now enter the family of states, and are socially and politically part and parcel of the Union.

We received, by this mail, ten days later news from all parts of the country than our latest dates from New York via Panama.

Mr. Ormsby, special correspondent of the New York Herald, was the only passenger from St. Louis by the stage . . .

[The above is part of an article which immediately follows Ormsby's, and, although not written by him, is of sufficient interest to be inserted here.]

[103] For an account of the mass meeting, at which Ormsby spoke, see San Francisco *Bulletin*, Oct. 11 and 12, 1858.

The Great Overland Mail

Special Correspondence of the New York Herald
San Francisco, Oct. 13, 1858

Conclusion of the Description of the Butterfield Route. The Road through Tucson, Fort Yuma, and Fort Tejon to San Francisco. The Colorado River, Deserts, Plains, and Mountain Passes. Condensed Table of Time, Rate of Speed, and Distances. Incidents by the Way. Jottings from a Wagon Seat, &c., &c., &c.

BY THE overland mail, from this point to St. Louis, of 11th inst., I advised you of the arrival of the great mail from St. Louis in twenty-three days and twenty-three hours and a half, and continued a description of the route as far as Tucson. I send herewith the description of the concluding portion of the route, from Tucson, through Fort Yuma, Los Angeles, and Fort Tejon, to San Francisco. I also gave you in that letter a table of the distances and time of departure from various points of the route, and a calculation of the rate of speed, which, in the haste of preparation for the next mail, after a long and fatiguing journey, was not as correct as it should have been. The mistake, however, was so obvious—making an error of 137 miles in the distance between Tucson and Fort Tejon —that any one at all acquainted with the route would discover it instantly. The following table is prepared with greater care, and may, I think, be relied on:

Overland Time Table Going West

Place	Miles Distant from Place to Place	Miles—Distance of Division	Time of Travelling Division D. H. M.	Av. Miles per Hour of Each Division	Time of Leaving Principal Station
St. Louis, Mo., and Memphis, Tenn.	–	–	–	–	Sep. 16 8 A.M.
P. R. R. terminus	160	–	–	–	" 16, 6:15 P.M.
Springfield, Mo.	143	–	–	–	" 17, 4 P.M.
Fayetteville, Ark.	100	–	–	–	" 18, 12 M.
Fort Smith	65	–	–	–	" 19, 3:30 A.M.
Sherman, Texas	205	673	4 8 40	6½	" 20, 4:40 P.M.
Ft. Belknap	146½	–	–	–	" 22, 7 A.M.
Ft. Chadbourne	136	282½	3 2 20	3¾	" 23, 7 P.M.
Franklin (opposite El Paso)	414	414	6 22 50	2½	" 30, 5:50 A.M.
Soldier's Farewell	150	–	–	–	Oct. 1, 10:15 A.M.
Tucson, Arizona	184½	334½	2 4 10	6½	" 2, 10 P.M.
Fort Tejon, Cal.	654	654	5 6 33	5¼	" 8, 4:33 A.M.
Visalia	127	–	–	–	" 8, 11:50 P.M.
Firebaugh's Ferry	82	–	–	–	" 9, 11:50 A.M.
Arrived at San Francisco	163	372	2 2 57	7¼	" 10, 7:30 A.M.
Totals		2,729½	23 23 30		

Thus the average rate of speed on the whole route was a fraction under five miles per hour.

Now, supposing that no better time than this is made, and not considering all the difficulties natural to a first trip, and more especially over a route, like this, which passes through nearly two thousand miles of uninhabited country, this route places San Francisco within twenty-six days of New York by mail and within twenty-four by mail and telegraph, affording by the semi-weekly stages communication between the bi-monthly departures of the steamers. But if the overland trip is made in twenty days— as it can be, and as I confidently predict it will be before the expiration of twelve months—this route places New York as convenient to San Francisco as the ordinary trips of the Pacific Mail Steamship Company. That the trip can be made in twenty days I have not the slightest doubt. The first trip had many difficulties which each succeeding trip will remove. Every month new stations will be built, shortening the relays of horses, and the roads will be much improved. Even with the very short time which has been made, there were distances varying from thirty to one hundred and thirteen miles travelled without relays of horses, except the *cavallados*, or droves—some of which I give below in tabular form:

Longest Distances of the First Overland Mail without Relays of Horses

Chadbourne, Texas, to Grape Creek, Texas, miles		30
Grape Creek, ”	Head of the Concho	50
Head of Concho, ”	Pecos River	75
Pecos River, ”	Pope's Camp	113
Pope's Camp, ”	Guadalupe Mountains	60
Guadalupe Pass, ”	Cornudas [Cornudos]	60
Pecatch [Picacho], Arizona,[104] to Cooke's Spring, Arizona		52
River Mimbres, ”	Soldier's Farewell	50
Soldier's Farewell, ”	Stein's Peak	42

These long distances between stations are through wild and uninhabited sections of country, where labor, timber, and all the appurtenances of stations have to be

[104] The stations noted in this table as being in Arizona were really in New Mexico.

conveyed, and to complete which time is required. But, as I said, the company is rapidly making preparations to build new stations between these long points, and some have doubtless been built and stocked already. A station was nearly finished on the 113 mile stretch up the Pecos River, about half way,[105] and part of the animals which we drove in the *cavallado* were left there for the next stage.

At the points where there is no water, if water cannot be obtained by digging it can be carried thence in the water carts or caught in tanks. An enterprising company is not to be frightened by trivial obstacles, and it will be a matter of economy with them to build stations in preference to killing their stock with such long and arduous drives. As to improving the roads, much has already been done. I have spoken in detail of the new road on Mr. Bates' route from Sherman, Texas, to Fort Belknap, Texas, which is thirty miles shorter than the old road, and now nearly as good. The new road from Grape Creek to the head of the Concho River, Texas, on Mr. Glover's division, is also in good order for travel and saves another thirty miles. The New Pass between Los Angeles, California, and Fort Tejon, California, has been much improved under the superintendence of Mr. M. L. Kinyon, as have also been other portions of the route. The route of the company will, of course, be a favorite emigrant route, and will, therefore, be kept in better order than before; in fact, each month will add new facilities to the overland mail.

[105] Ormsby refers to the camp, above Emigrant Crossing, that was in process of construction when the first stage went through. Farwell, the *Alta* correspondent, a month later, reported two more stations on the Pecos.

As I have frequently mentioned, the route needs thorough military protection. There are many places where a few resolute men could rifle the stage at will and possess themselves of a valuable mail. Instead of posting large bodies of men in comfortable quarters in populated districts, the government might advantageously distribute them along the route, where they might serve the double purpose of keeping the Indians in check and protecting the mail from desperate white men, who are none the less to be feared. This done, the speedy growth of settlements along the line will be secured and the certainty and regularity of the trips insured. The military posts, being on the mail route, will have speedy communication with each other, so that the forces may almost instantaneously be concentrated at any given point, instead of, as now, requiring months for the transmission of orders and the transportation of troops. A wall will be erected along the frontier, on the line of which settlements will grow, and beyond which the blood-thirsty Indians will not be allowed to pass.

Accommodations for Passengers

Since my stay in San Francisco I have had many inquiries as to the means of procuring meals and sleeping, along the route, for individuals about to traverse it. Of course these are not to be procured as comfortably as in the Astor House or our own houses, and for much of the distance the traveller has to rough it in the roughest manner. From Red River to El Paso there are few accommodations for eating, beyond what are afforded by the company stations to their own employees. In time, arrangements will be made to supply good meals at these points. The first travellers will find it convenient to carry with them as much durable food as possible. As for sleeping, most of the wagons are arranged so that the backs of the seats let down and form a bed the length of the vehicle. When the stage is full, the passengers must take turns at sleeping. Perhaps the jolting will be found disagreeable at first, but a few nights without sleeping will obviate that difficulty, and soon the jolting will be as little of a disturbance as the rocking of a cradle to a sucking babe. For my part, I found no difficulty in sleeping over the roughest roads, and I have no doubt that any one else will learn quite as quickly. A bounce of the wagon, which makes one's head strike the top, bottom, or sides, will be equally disregarded, and "nature's sweet restorer" found as welcome on the hard bottom of the wagon as in the downy beds of the St. Nicholas. White pants and kid gloves had better be discarded by most passengers.

The Employees

The employees of the company, I found, without exception, to be courteous, civil, and attentive. They are most of them from the East, and many, especially of the drivers, from New York state. I found the drivers on the whole line, with but few exceptions, experienced men. Several are a little reckless and too anxious to make fast time, but as a general thing they are very cautious.

All the superintendents are experienced stage men: Mr. Crocker, who has charge of the division from St. Louis and Memphis to Red River, has his line in excellent condition; Mr. Bates, from Red River to Chadbourne, has worked very hard, especially with his new road and wild mules, and is an old stage man; Mr. Glover, from Chadbourne to the Rio Grande, has a very wild and unsettled country under his charge, and his arrangements were not very complete yet, but, as I have said, this portion of the road will grow better every month; Messrs. Hawley & Buckley, from El Paso to Los Angeles, are both experienced stage men who will attend to their business; Mr. Kinyon (who, like Mr. Hawley, is one of the owners) is, as the perfectness of the arrangements on his end of the line indicate, an experienced stage man.

The road agents, or sub-superintendents, are also, all of them, men of much experience, and the company appears to have taken every care to have their employees reliable. Considering that the contract was signed but just a year before the route went into operation; that an exploring party had to be sent over the road to lay out the details of the line, consuming nearly eight months' time; that during this time over 100 wagons had to be built, nearly 1,500 horses and mules bought and stationed, corrals and station houses built, men employed, and all these appurtenances disposed along the route—the work appears to me to be superhuman. Then it must be taken into consideration that food and clothing for all these men and horses have to be transported over the line, which is no mean item in itself.

I have thus far given you a description of the route as far as Tucson, and, with this, finish that part of my labors. I have no doubt that the work is feasible, that the route will be successful, that passengers to the western states and from thence to California will patronize it, that the towns along the route will improve and others spring up, that military protection will be extended, that new mining districts will be discovered and worked, that the great work

of the Pacific railroad will be forwarded, that the people
of California will have regular information from the East
twice per week, and that the contractors will realize handsomely on the investments which they make in this great
enterprise of the day.

Resuming my narrative where I left off in my last, I
find myself at Tucson.

Description of the Route Resumed

Tucson[106] is a small place, consisting of a few adobe
houses. The inhabitants are mainly Mexicans. There are
but few Americans, though they keep the two or three
stores and are elected to the town offices. The town has
considerably improved since the acquisition of the territory by the United States. The Apache Indians are somewhat troublesome in the vicinity. We left the town on
Saturday, October 2, having to drive forty miles to the
next station, in the Pecacho [Picacho] Pass,[107] before we
came to desirable water. There had been a recent rain,
however, and we found water for our animals on the
route, scooping it up from little ponds by the roadside.
The road was over a plain covered with the customary
wild vegetation of the country, but through no settlements. The pass is through one of the scattered mountains

[106] Now the county seat of Pima County. "Name comes from the Piman
'Sluyk-son,' meaning dark or brown spring . . . There is little doubt that
it became a Spanish settlement not earlier than 1776. Before that time it
was a Ranchería, probably of mixed Pima, Papago, and Sobaipuri peoples."
The capital of the Territory of Arizona was moved from Prescott to
Tucson, Nov. 1, 1857, and moved back to Prescott in 1877. (Barnes, *Arizona
Place Names*, p. 455.)

[107] Bailey records a station called "Pointer Mountain (Charcos de los
Pimos)" between Tucson and Picacho Pass. Barnes (*op. cit.*, p. 341) calls
it "Point of Mountain."

of the Sierra Madre range, and is not particularly different
from ordinary mountain roads.

The Pimos [Pima] Indians

Forty miles beyond the pass the company have a station,
where I saw the first Indians in their wild native costume
—much resembling that of our New York model artists.
They were a band of fifteen Pimos [Pima], engaged in
dressing a beeve which they had just sold to the station
keeper. The dexterity with which they separated the
various parts and sliced up the animal into strings of meat
to be dried was quite remarkable. The men were generally
in the costume of Adam, with a dirty cloth in the place
of the fig leaf. The women, of which there were three,
had cloths slightly larger, and a little cleaner, but down to
the middle of the body wore beads on their necks and
arms, and "didn't wear anything else." They all of them
had fine muscular developements and were the very picture of health.

Two or three of the men had their faces and bodies
painted, having just returned from the war path. It appeared that the Apaches had a few days since gone into
their camp in large numbers and stolen a few of their
cattle, and they had been following the trail, though without success. Their faces were painted an ebony black and
their lips of a deep red color, so that I at first thought they
were blacks, as they lay basking in the sun or sleeping in
the shade. Some of the band lounged about and looked on
with curiosity as we changed our horses and partook of
our breakfast.

This station was located on the Gila River,[108] near the

[108] Sacaton. Barnes (p. 372) says it is a very old Indian settlement, and
the seat of the Pima and Maricopa Indian agency.

range of mountains known as the Casa Grande. A few miles beyond we came to the Pimos [Pima] villages, scattered along the Gila on a reservation of fifteen square miles. The land here is rich and, with irrigation, produces bountiful crops. The Pimos [Pima] number in all about 22,000.[109] They raise corn and wheat in very large quantities, which they sell to the whites. Their houses are miserable huts, built of mesquite bushes or hoops covered with straw.

The Indians are hideous looking objects in their filthy scraps of clothing and naked brown bodies, and frequently frightened our mules as they passed by. The men are lazy and take good care to make the women do all the work. We saw numbers of sovereign lords walking along, or riding, and making their squaws carry the loads—a spectacle which would give one of our women's rights women fits instanter. The women are, however, lazy too, and the men have about as much work to drive them as they would to do the work themselves. The price of hay, of which there is but comparatively little raised here, is from $15 to $20 per ton. Corn and wheat sell at from two to three cents per pound.[110]

The Maricopas [Maricopa] Wells

Twenty-four miles from our last station we came to the Maricopas [Maricopa] Wells, situated in a large plain of alkali soil and coarse grass. There are, in all, six or eight

[109] Ormsby's estimate is too high, as the census the following year recorded only 3,770 Pima. See Report of the Commissioner of Indian Affairs . . . for the Year 1859 (Washington, 1860), p. 360.

[110] "They [the Pima] have under fence and in cultivation 15,000 acres of land this year, an increase of one-third over last. They have this year disposed of, to the trading posts, 220,000 pounds of wheat, at two cents per pound." (Ibid.)

wells, and the water is very good. We found a number of Indians there, and one of them had the audacity to ask me three bits (37½ cents) for a small melon which he wished to sell. I showed him two three-cent pieces, and the look of insufferable contempt which he gave me would be worth a fortune to an actor if put in in the right place. I am sure his melon would rot before he could get another chance to sell it.

A Forty Mile Desert

From the Maricopas [Maricopa] Wells, where we changed our horses for a mule team, we had a forty mile ride over the corner of a vast desert. The soil was coarse sand and gravel, and the road excellent. No water can be found the entire distance. I here saw some of the largest cactus plants on the route; they tower up from twelve to fifteen feet in some of the varieties. A very excellent and sweet syrup is made from them. The stalks, which are very tough, are sometimes used for building huts.

We arrived at the station on the Gila River—which is a time table station—at the edge of the forty mile desert, on Sunday, October 3, at 9:30 P.M., and left at ten, our road now running along the northern [i.e., southern] banks of the Gila to Fort Yuma on the Colorado, about 100 miles from its mouth. The stations in the Gila Valley are from fifteen to twenty miles apart. The first we touched at was called "Murderer's Grave." It was the scene of the summary killing of a young man by a band of emigrants, he having in a fit of passion shot a guardian who had him in charge. His punishment was as summary as his crime, and his wealth did not avail him to escape, as perhaps it might in a more "civilized and enlightened community."

Fifteen miles further on we came to "Oatman Flats [Flat]," the burial place of the unfortunate Oatman family, whose sad story has been published in book form within a year.[111] They were part of an emigrant train, and from some cause had become separated from the rest. They were met in this lonely spot by a band of Apaches, and the whole family left for dead, with the exception of two young girls who were carried off by the Indians. The son, however, survived his wounds and succeeded in crawling many miles to a ranche. After an arduous search of two years he finally recovered one of his sisters by paying a heavy ransom, and discovered that the other had died during her captivity.[112] The graves of the father and mother are directly in the road, and the teams often pass over them. They lie some distance from the scene of the murder, which took place on a hill half a mile off. Mr. Jacobs, the road agent on this section of the line, intends having the graves enclosed with a fence, so as to turn the road aside.

Experience En Route

The hill on which the murder was committed is very steep and covered with deep sand. It has been partly repaired by Colonel Leach but is still a very difficult place for heavy teams and no easy one for light ones. There

[111] Ormsby probably refers to R. B. Stratton's *Life among the Indians: Being an Interesting Narrative of the Captivity of the Oatman Girls, among the Apache and Mohave Indians* (San Francisco, 1857).

[112] The family of Royce Oatman was attacked by the Apache-Mohave Indians on Mar. 28, 1851. One girl, Mary Ann, died in captivity the following year. Olive, the elder, was rescued in 1856, and returned to her brother at Fort Yuma. (Barnes, p. 305; Stratton, *op. cit.*)

are several very bad hills between the Oatman Flats [Flat] and the "Dutchman,"[113] a station on the Gila, about twenty-two miles distant, where we took breakfast and enjoyed the luxury of a bath. A ride of eighteen miles over a rough, stony, and sandy road brought us to Texas Hill, near Pringle's Peak, a rugged mount, about 1,500 feet high, which tapers down to the level of the plain, into which it juts like the nose of a sword fish. It is mainly composed of red slate rocks, and in the moonlight looks like a hill of icebergs.

I had expected to get supper at the next station, but, it not being ready, and Mr. Warren Hall, the road agent, being anxious to get the mail along in time, I had to content myself with a pipe and a glass of water, and ride along, although I had had nothing to eat since breakfast. But we had a good road and a fast team, and came along finely. Indeed, since leaving Tucson our teams had been far better than on the other end of the route, and, as you must have observed by the table, our rate of speed was much greater. The line is exceedingly well stocked from Tucson to San Francisco, and but few mules are used. Were it not for the excellence of the stock and arrangements of the stations on this end of the line, the first mail could not have come through in time.

At a station twenty miles from Fort Yuma[114] we met the fourth stage from San Francisco, thirty hours ahead of time, waiting for us to come up, to change stages. They had a full load of passengers, including a man, his wife, and two children, who were going through to Mem-

[113] Bailey records this as Flap-jack ranch.

[114] Swiveller's ranch. Between Flap-jack and Swiveller's, Bailey records three stations: Griswell's, Peterman's, and Fillibuster camp.

phis. The woman and children stood the fatigue of the trip bravely. As for the exchange of stages, we got rather the worst of it, as we had to take a lumber wagon and patch up the harness with ropes. Mr. Hall, the road agent, is, however, a man of much energy, and soon set matters straight, and I believe we made quite as good time to Fort Yuma in our lumber wagon as we had made before.

Mr. Hall is an old stage man, having been concerned in some of the first stage lines of California[115] and engaged in the business since 1849. He has been engaged, under the direction of Mr. Kinyon, in stocking the line from Tucson to Los Angeles, and has secured some of the finest stage teams on the route. Our rate of speed on his division was about five and a half miles per hour, which was very good, considering the sandy desert we had to traverse.

Fort Yuma is now in command of Colonel Flourney,[116] with fifteen men. It is situated on the Colorado—west bank —near its junction with the Gila. Most of the buildings belong to the government.[117] About a mile below the fort

[115] Warren F. Hall commenced his California stage-line activities in 1850. In that year he and Jared B. Crandall purchased the Whistman stage line— San Francisco to San José. See O. O. Winther, *Express and Stagecoach Days in California* (Stanford University, 1938), pp. 82-94, *passim;* H. C. Ward, "Stage-Coach Days in California: Reminiscences of H. C. Ward," ed. O. O. Winther, in Calif. Hist. Soc. *Quart.,* XIII, 255-61.

[116] No record of Colonel Flourney has been found. The San Francisco *Bulletin* correspondent, in his letter from Fort Yuma, Oct. 30, 1858, says, "There are three companies of U. S. Artillery, viz: F, H, and J, numbering in all 180 men—the companies not being full. Col. Nauman is in command of this post." (San Francisco *Bulletin,* Nov. 8, 1858.) The colonel was George Nauman (1803?-63). See Cullum, *Biographical Register,* I, 304-5.

[117] Fort Yuma, Calif., was established as an army post on Nov. 27, 1850, and first called "Post at the Mouth of the Gila," or "Military Post at the Junction of the Gila and Colorado Rivers." It was named Fort Yuma sometime in 1852. See Eugene Bandel, *Frontier Life in the Army, 1854-1861,* tr.

is Arizona City, consisting of a few adobe houses.[118] We crossed the river at this point, on the ferry kept by Mr. Yager,[119] who charges $5 for carrying an ordinary four horse team. The boat is a sort of flatboat, and is propelled by the rapid current, being kept in its course by pulleys running on a rope stretched across the river. We crossed just at daybreak and found the few Americans ready to receive us. After a hasty breakfast we changed our horses and were off again.

The Colorado River

Our road for ten miles ran along the banks of the Colorado, which is navigable for steamers of very light draught up to this point. The river takes an abrupt sweep from east to west here, which is gradually wearing away the western bank to a great extent—so much so that the road is in many places washed away. The road leads through heavy sand and bushes. The quicksands are very large and shift with much rapidity, often building an island in a spot which a few hours before was the centre of the channel. The land in the vicinity of the river is very fertile and can easily be made to produce all kinds of

---

Olga Bandel and Richard Jente, ed. R. P. Bieber ("The Southwest Historical Series," II; Glendale, Calif., 1932), pp. 260-63.

[118] Arizona City was located and surveyed in 1854, but first called Colorado City. In 1873, by an act of the Arizona territorial legislature, the name was changed to Yuma. See Barnes, pp. 499-500.

[119] Louis John Frederick Yager (Jaeger, or Iaeger), in the summer of 1850, organized a company of twelve men to operate the ferry. Yager continued in business at this point until 1877. See B. A. Stephens, "A Biographical Sketch of L. J. F. Iaeger," in Hist. Soc. of Sou. Calif. *Annual Publications*, I [pt. 4] (1889), pp. 36-40; "Diary of a Ferryman and Trader at Fort Yuma, 1855-1857," ed. G. W. Beattie, *ibid.*, XIV, pts. 1 and 2 (1928-29), pp. 89-128, 213-42.

vegetable growth. About ten miles from the fort is Pilot Knob,[120] a mountain which extends nearly to the very verge of the river, leaving but a narrow pass for the road.

The road from Fort Yuma, for fifty miles west, runs through the northwest corner of Mexico. At Fort Yuma we leave the Gadsden Purchase through the southern edge of Arizona, whose mineral resources are her best recommendation. The California line is just below Fort Yuma; and it is to avoid a bad part of the sandy desert that the road is kept through Mexico or Lower California. I should have stated, before, that we met Colonel Leach's train at Fort Yuma, en route for San Diego, having finished work on the roads.

The mail route was laid out to run through San Bernardino, through whose fertile district it is most desirable that it should run; but the great difficulty of getting over ninety-three miles of a waterless, heavy, sandy road could not be overcome, and the old road through the upper corner of Mexico is preserved.[121]

The California Desert

For full sixty miles the sand is extremely heavy, and progress with loaded teams very difficult. Near the road is a steep sand hill, with little or no vegetation, which extends sixty miles into the plain. A few days before we left Fort Yuma (which was on Tuesday, the 5th, at 6:15 A.M.), there had been a heavy sand storm on the desert. Some of the sand drifts were very high, and in many cases

[120] Bailey lists a station at Pilot Knob.

[121] For information concerning the efforts made to route the Overland Mail Company's line through San Bernardino Valley, see G. W. and H. P. Beattie, *Heritage of the Valley: San Bernardino's First Century* (Pasadena, 1939), pp. 339-45.

the road was entirely covered up. These sand storms are very violent, and often men and animals are lost in them. On one occasion a wealthy cattle owner of California lost three thousand head of sheep in six hours; and out of 6,000 sheep, with which he started for San Francisco, from Chadbourne, Texas, he only reached his point of destination with 1,500.

On our way we met several small companies of Yuma Indians, crossing the desert on foot, carrying their water gourds. The Yumas are a peaceably disposed tribe, and these did us no more harm than to make faces at us and grin as our horses shied from them. I found the journey quite unpleasant enough in the wagon; but they seemed to enjoy the walk, as if they were used to it. We took the precaution to keep a sharp lookout on our back boot, where the baggage was kept, so as to leave them no temptation to steal—a temptation which they would not be likely to resist.

Twenty-four miles of pretty rough riding through the sand brought us to one of the company's stations, kept by a kind hearted gentleman named Elliott, who only charges one dollar for a meal of crackers, pork, and coffee. We found that there were no horses ready for us at the station; but, fortunately, an agent of the San Diego Mail Company was passing with a lot of stock, and Mr. Hall soon made a trade with him for a team, and we suffered no detention. I thought at first that he had much the worst of the bargain, for one old mare insisted on pulling the wrong way. They all finally pulled together, however, through the excellent management of Mr. Hall, and we started on another twenty-four mile ride, to the Indian Wells. Mr. Elliott's station was called Alamo Mocho, or the cottonwood stump. The stump must have been covered up in the sand, for I could not see it.[122]

New River

A few miles beyond we crossed New River, which is indicated on the maps, but has never been seen but once, which was by a military expedition in 1851. They camped at night, supposing they were a great distance from water, and in the morning, to their surprise, found they were on the banks of a river. Many reasons were at first assigned for it; some said that it was a large spring, and others that it was a series of springs. I believe, however, the final conclusion was that it was a sort of slough from the Colorado, for it shortly disappeared, leaving in its bed vast numbers of fine fish, whose decaying bodies made the most horrid stench for months. It went almost as quickly as it came.

Indian Wells—A Creek in the Sand

Twenty-four miles of heavy sand riding brought us to the Indian Wells, where we found the station men had had some difficulty with Indians, who refused to let them have water for their animals. Almost a collision ensued, but the Indians finally retired without making an attack, although they were vastly in the majority. Twenty-four miles from the wells we came to Carisso [Carrizo] Creek, which is indicated on the maps, but, as it appeared to us, was a simple sandy gully, a little damp. Our road for a considerable distance lay directly in its bed—was indeed a desolate one. The vegetation within sight was of but

[122] Bailey records a station—Cook's Wells—between Pilot Knob and Alamo Mocho.

little account, while not a tree could be seen except upon
the distant mountains, where there are many fine cattle
ranches; but we could see nothing of vegetation but here
and there a clump of mesquite, or some other wild bush
of the plains.

Cattle Dying of Thirst

An emigrant train had just passed, and we met numbers
of cattle which had been abandoned as being too weak
to travel; there they stood, almost living skeletons, gradually dying of thirst, with water within a few miles of
them. I could almost imagine they looked supplicatingly
at us and begged for just one single drop. Some were
standing, others lying, and others just gasping in the ago-
nies of death—a sight almost enough to sicken the stoutest
heart. The loss to emigrant trains, especially large ones,
is very great from this cause. Very often one half or two
thirds of a large drove of cattle will have to be left on
the road, too weak to proceed, from want of water. The
Indians gather up these stray cattle by carrying water to
them or driving them to the nearest creek, as, by the cus-
tom of the country, cattle thus picked up are seldom re-
claimed by their original owners.

One of the greatest benefits of the establishment of this
overland mail route will be that it will indicate to the
emigrant, with his valuable droves of cattle, the safest and
surest means of transit across these waterless plains, which
are so little travelled that disputes often occur among
directors of a train as to which is the right road. I was
furnished with a sad illustration of this fact by a passenger
in our stage from Pilot Knob to El Monte (a distance of
280 miles), who paid almost his last cent for passage

money for himself and family of wife and two children —one a fat, hearty infant but eight months of age, whose joyous glee was quite an addition to our company on the tedious road, besides being a reminder of another little one more than two thousand miles away.

The passenger of whom I speak had started with a large emigrant train from Fort Chadbourne, Texas, to cross the great Staked Plain, the crossing of which I described in my last. A dispute arose as to the proper course; most of the party contended for striking a northern course, but he and another, who had crossed the plains several times, insisted that they should steer west and strike the Pecos. They were, however, overruled, and the train passed directly across the plain roads leading to water. The consequence was that there were three thousand head of cattle left to die a terrible death on the plain from thirst, adding their bones to the vast numbers which whiten it and line the roadside, their grim skeletons warning the traveller of the dreadful dangers of the desert. The passenger's name was Foreman, of Williamson County, Texas, and when he left the stage at El Monte he was so altered by the fatigue of his journey that his own sister did not know him.

California Valleys

The company have a station at Carisso [Carrizo] Creek, where plenty of water can be had by digging. About half way between the next [i.e., this] station and Vallecito is Palm Spring, so called on account of a number of palm plants which grow near it; we met the fifth stage from San Francisco, which was a little behind the usual time but ahead of schedule time. Vallecito, or Little Valley, is a beautiful green spot—a perfect oasis in the desert; it is about five miles square, surrounded by rugged timberless hills, and the green bushes and grass and hard road are a most refreshing relief from the sandy sameness of the desert. There are a number of springs, some of them salt. There is but one ranche, where we changed horses. The sand sparkles in the sun with large quantities of mica, which the uninitiated often mistake for gold dust, as it much resembles the precious metal in color. We found, here, part of Mr. Foreman's emigrant train, which from thirty-three wagons had dwindled down to seven, with but a tithe of the cattle with which they started.

From Little Valley the road leads, through a rough cañon, over a steep and stony hill into another valley, whose only characteristic is an abundance of grease weed [greasewood], which whether wet or dry is excellent fuel. At the end of this valley, twenty-eight miles from Vallecito, our road strikes the San Diego road, and proceeds through a very narrow pass—the most wonderful on the route.[123] It appears to have been the bed of a fierce torrent, but it was now dry. The channel appears to have been cut through the solid rocks with the regularity of a deep cut for a railroad, and perpendicularly up the steep sides of the narrow pass the jagged rocks tower, apparently ready to fall and crush all beneath them. Yet among these jagged peaks there are many varieties of curious weeds—cactus plants, Spanish dagger, prickly pear, and maguey—from which nutricious food and drink is obtained. From the maguey plant an exhilarating liquor, called "mescal," is made, while the plant itself, after being baked for twenty-four hours, affords an excellent meal.

[123] Box Canyon.

The outer covering of the leaf, which somewhat resembles the Spanish dagger, is also, I believe, used for making a rope, as the fibres are much like hemp. The mountains near the road abound in mica and are no doubt replete with mineral wealth.

Our progress through this portion of the road was quite slow, necessarily, and it required all Mr. Hall's skill to guide our team and wagon safely through the pass, for in some places there was hardly an inch to spare. It is the most wonderful natural road I ever saw or heard of; one of the drivers, however, thought the journey rather dull and declared that, if God ever pronounced this part of the earth good, it was more than ever man did. Mr. Foreman suggested that God knew what was in the mountains and man did not; but he was met by the assurance that the mountains were of little good to man, since he didn't know what was in them. To me it seemed a special dispensation of Providence to make us the more appreciate the beautiful road which lay just beyond, for, just as we came up from the rugged pass, we struck a beautiful hard road which would rival the Third Avenue in its palmiest days.

Pleasant Sights

It seemed to infuse new life into ourselves and animals, and I felt as if I could at that moment turn back and cheerfully re-traverse the dreary journey which I had passed, in consideration of this little patch of good road. It led directly across the bed of a large lake, now dry, but which in forcing an outlet had evidently cut the deep pass through which we had just come. We were now fairly out of the desert, and from this point until we reach San Francisco—a distance of over seven hundred miles—the route is through a series of fertile valleys, abounding in fruits and agricultural productions, compared with which the gold fields of the state sink into insignificance.

In the valley of San Felipe we saw a number of prosperous Indian ranches, where they raise corn and melons and live much like white folks. Warner's ranche is a comfortable house, situated in the valley, in the midst of a beautiful meadow, and with its shingled roof looked more like civilization than anything I had seen for many days. There were hundreds of cattle grazing on the plain, and everything looked as comfortable as every natural advantage could secure.[124] Our road lay through some delightful oak groves—a most decided improvement on the desert —while the cool, delicious springs of water were most acceptable. The stations (through these valleys of Buena Vista), Hall's Oak Grove, Swango [Aguanga], Laguna, and Temacula [Temecula],[125] are all at convenient distances, and the accommodations excellent, and the road is

[124] The ranch was owned by Juan José Warner (1807-95), better known to the Spaniards as Juan Largo. He was born Jonathan Trumbull Warner but changed his name sometime after his arrival in California in 1831. As a naturalized Mexican citizen he twice petitioned the government for grants of land, and received in 1845 El Valle de San José, and in 1846 an additional "four square leagues" adjoining the first grant. See J. J. Hill, *The History of Warner's Ranch and Its Environs* (Los Angeles, 1927), pp. 94-111.

[125] Temecula precedes Laguna, which was also known as Laguna Grande, and is now called Lake Elsinore. For information concerning the station at Laguna see J. W. Gould, "The Butterfield Stage Station at 'Laguna Grande,'" in *Hist. Soc. of Sou. Calif. Quart.*, XVIII, 46-49.

The next station was Temescal but not mentioned by Ormsby. For information concerning the station see Frank Rolfe, "The Location of the Butterfield Station in the Temescal Valley, Riverside County," *ibid.*, XVII, 108-11.

lined with prosperous ranches. Through San Diego County the verdure was quite luxuriant, owing to the recent rains.

Our road lay through a valley in the southwest corner of San Bernardino County, having the San Bernardino Mountains on the east and the coast range on the west. The land is rich and could produce everything, but it lies almost uncultivated, being used principally for grazing. The owners prefer to grow rich without doing any work. They have plenty of meat ready at hand and can buy what they want by selling stock. Many of them buy wheat and corn, while their lands would produce abundant crops with the greatest ease. Our road leads through Chino ranche—the richest in San Bernardino County—the proprietor of which is estimated to own about $300,000 worth of cattle, yet at our breakfast, here, we had neither butter nor milk, without which the merest hod carrier in New York would think his meal incomplete. Their cattle dot the plains for miles around, and their land could produce everything; but they have not even the comforts of a Massachusetts farmer among his rocky hills.[126]

I could not but think what a different spectacle these fertile valleys would present were they peopled by some of our sturdy, industrious eastern farmers, and I recurred to my reflection in the Mesilla Valley, that Providence

[126] Chino ranch was owned by the daughters of Isaac Williams, who died in 1856 and who was the son-in-law of Antonio María Lugo, original grantee. The daughters married two Americans, John Rains and Robert S. Carlisle. Rains was manager of the ranch until Carlisle bought Mrs. Rains's share in 1859. See G. W. and H. P. Beattie, *Heritage of the Valley*, pp. 120-37.

For a brief history of the stations between Chino and Los Angeles, see R. M. Fryer, "The Butterfield Stage Route," in Hist. Soc. of Sou. Calif. *Quart.*, XVII, 15-22.

knew just where to locate the lazy men and the industrious ones. Perhaps it is the very luxuriance of the soil, and the ease with which anything can be produced, that makes the people insensible to the benefits which they have; but to me it seemed a great pity to see so much good land useless.

San Bernardino County—Rich Ranches

After crossing the Santa Ana River in San Bernardino County, the road runs through the Chino ranche, which is marked on Colton's map, though it consists of but one house. The course is then due west into Los Angeles County, which may well be called "The Angels'" county, for the rich fertility of its soil. A few miles before reaching Los Angeles city, we pass through the beautiful little town of El Monte, which is ranged along the road for nearly five miles, and is composed of a series of neat looking houses built of wood, and considerable cultivated land. The fences are, many of them, "live fence," made by planting cottonwood, poplar, or willow, much like the eastern willow, which soon grows to a large size and lines the road for miles. The post office is a wooden building, with a neat piazza and shingled roof, which looked quite refreshing after over a thousand miles' travel without seeing a house having the appearance of civilization.[127] The roads through this county are excellent, and as we ride along we pass numerous herds of cattle. Many of these herds are watched by dogs, which are so well trained

[127] Bailey records a station called San José, between Chino and El Monte. El Monte, the oldest American settlement in Los Angeles County, was the end of the trail for many covered-wagon emigrants. It was founded about 1851. See Fryer, *op. cit.*, p. 17; Harris Newmark, *Sixty Years in Southern California, 1853-1913*, ed. M. H. and M. R. Newmark (2d ed.; New York, 1926), pp. 90-92.

that they keep the flocks together and will not permit strange men or ravenous animals to approach.

Trained Dogs

One man in this county has three dogs who take the herds from the corral in the morning, drive them to good pasturage, and watch them until night, when they bring them back. They take turns at meal times, two remaining while the third goes home to his meal. This may seem a pretty tough story, but I am assured that it is a fact.

Los Angeles

Los Angeles city is about twenty-seven miles from the coast, on the San Pedro River.[128] It contains about 6,000 inhabitants, and has a number of fine buildings. The people are mostly Mexicans, Spanish, and Indians, but, since the acquisition of the state by the United States, the Americans have been increasing in numbers.[129] There is a weekly paper published there,[130] and the town, as I passed through it, looked thrifty and business-like. On the outskirts of the city are the vineyards, covering many acres and producing the most luscious grapes, from which wines are made which have a world-wide celebrity. Celebrated sparkling wines are made here. The fruits of the neighborhood are of the largest kind. I saw some pears

[128] Should read Los Angeles River.

[129] Los Angeles was founded Sept. 4, 1781, by Felipé de Neve, the Spanish governor of California. Its full name was Pueblo de Nuestra Señora la Reina de los Angeles de Porciúncula.
According to the 8th census of the United States (1860), the population of the city was divided as follows: 3,854 whites, 66 colored, 446 Indians, 10 half-breeds, 9 Asiatic; total, 4,385.

[130] There were three weekly papers at that time: the *Los Angeles Star*, *Southern Vineyard*, and *El Clamor Publico*.

which would take premiums at our agricultural fairs. Their flavor was, however, inferior to the Bartlett pear.

We arrived at Los Angeles in five days and four hours from Tucson, making nearly six miles an hour on the average, in spite of the sandy desert and craggy hills. As we entered the town we met the sixth mail from San Francisco, which left on Monday, October 4, with two through passengers. We stopped only long enough to change coaches, and started on our way again. We met here Mr. M. L. Kinyon, the superintendent of this end of the road, through whose energy the line from Tucson all the way to San Francisco has been stocked. Messrs. Hawley and Buckley, the superintendents between El Paso and Los Angeles, received much assistance from him, and he was much aided by Mr. Warren Hall, of whom I have before spoken as an experienced stage man. The stock from Los Angeles is very good, and we made the best time on that part of the route—sometimes making twelve miles per hour, including stoppages. He has some excellent drivers, and his longest station is twenty-six miles. The average distance between the relays of horses is from ten to fifteen miles.

The Route beyond Los Angeles

Our first change was nine miles from Los Angeles.[131] Fifteen miles further we changed at the old Spanish mission of San Fernando, which is marked on Colton's map.[132] It was built for the Indians and consists of a number of

[131] Cahuenga. For brief information concerning the stations between Los Angeles and Tule River station, now Porterville, see H. A. Spindt, "The Butterfield Stage Route from Los Angeles to Porterville," in Hist. Soc. of Sou. Calif. *Quart.*, XVIII, 41-45.

[132] Mission San Fernando Rey de España was founded on Sept. 8, 1797.

low ranches; the remains indicate that it was once a fine adobe building, with large pillars in front and a fine belfry and fountain. A niche in the centre of the building contains a fine piece of old statuary. Part of the building is now used as a stable for the company's horses; and the only inhabitants we saw were a few Indian women, washing in a little brook which gurgles by, who giggled in high glee as we passed with our beautiful team of six white horses—two more than our usual allowance, in consideration of a heavy cañon and pass which lay in our route. It would be well for other portions of the road east of El Paso if six horse teams were used, as there are in a number of difficult places, such as the Colorado Desert and the Pecatcho [Picacho] Pass; but I suppose a little time will regulate all these matters.

The road leads through the New Pass,[132a] where it strikes the old road from San Bernardino to the Tejon Pass of the Sierra Nevada mountains. The cañon road is rugged and difficult. About the centre of the pass is, I believe, the steepest hill on the whole route. I should judge it to be full 800 feet from the level of the road, which has to be ascended and descended in the space of a quarter of a mile. Perhaps my idea of the distance is not correct; but certainly it is a very steep hill, and our six horses found great difficulty in drawing our empty wagon up. The road takes some pretty sharp turns in the cañon, and a slight accident might precipitate a wagon load into a very uncomfortable abyss. At the base of the cañon is the smooth sandy bed of a creek, which was now dry.

[132a] Ormsby means San Fernando Pass. He repeats this error on pp. 92, 123. New Pass, named by Lt. Williamson, was located southeast of San Francisquito Canyon.

Eight miles from San Fernando we changed horses again, at Hart's ranch, having made nearly ten miles per hour, and in spite of the bad condition of the roads, after one of the heaviest rains ever known in the county. From this point the road leads through the San Francisco [Francisquito] Cañon, twelve miles long, the small jagged peaks of the mountains on either side looking much like rows of upturned human profiles. We reached Fort Tejon,[133] ninety-six miles from Los Angeles, at 3:40 A.M. on Friday, Oct. 8, where we again struck the route mentioned in the published time table.

Fort Tejon

Fort Tejon is directly in the pass and has some very fine adobe buildings, most of which belong to the government.[134] There are few settlers. The price of hay, here, is $43 per ton, and barley six cents per pound. I should think some of our enterprising Yankees, who think ten dollars per ton for hay a very high price, could make fortunes, here, if they could only get the liberty of cultivating a few of the many acres of now useless fertile lands in this section of California. We left the fort at 4:33 A.M., our route passing through Grape [Grapevine] Cañon. The hills on either side of this cañon have a remarkably round and smooth appearance. The road is winding and verges on many a dangerous precipice, requiring the most careful and experienced drivers. The road through the pass for

[133] Bailey lists four stations between Hart's and Fort Tejon: King's, Widow Smith's, French John's, and Reed's.

[134] Fort Tejon was established on Aug. 10, 1854, and abandoned Sept. 11, 1864. Hamersly, *Complete Regular Army Register*, Pt. II, p. 156. See also H. G. Comfort, *Where Rolls the Kern* (Moorpark, Calif., 1934), pp. 21-52.

five miles is good, and then we strike a level plain, for thirteen miles, to the Sink of Tejon, the next station, at the entrance of the pass.

The next station is sixteen miles distant,[135] and the road across a plain, with some heavy sand and one or two steep hills. Fifteen miles from the last station we cross the Kern River, which empties into the Tulare Lake. We are now in a vast plain, through which our road runs for one hundred miles, crossing a series of rivers and creeks which empty into the Tulare Lake. The Kern River is a rapid running stream, and has to be crossed on boats. A man named Gordon[136] keeps the ferry and has a large flatboat which being out of order, at this time, the stages could not cross and we had to cross in a small boat propelled stern first, with a shovel, by the dexterous hand of the ferryman. The company have a station here, and no detention is experienced as horses and another wagon are waiting on the other side. The land along the river bottom is good.

We have now to cross thirty-three miles of sandy road over some steep foothills of the Sierra Nevada, with only an occasional green spot to relieve the monotony. For several miles the road winds at the foot of these hills, with abrupt turns which keep a team travelling like horses in a circus ring, though the curves are alternately to the right and to the left. The hills are barren. Occasionally we have a steep one, and from the top can see, as far as the eye can reach, nothing but the tops of other hills and the craggy summit of the Sierra Nevada. The two or three little groves of mesquite, poplar, and cottonwood are quite

[135] Kern River Slough.

[136] Major Gordon ran the ferry on the Kern River from 1854 to 1859. (Spindt, *op. cit.,* p. 42.)

a relief, and you wonder, as you look at the sandy soil, how even the sage bushes can live. All that we saw of King's River was its dry bed, and I passed it without knowing it.[137] There is, however, a pump to mark the spot. We stopped at stations at Pose [Poso] Creek, twenty-six miles from King's River, seven miles thence at White River, and eighteen miles thence to the next station.[138]

Visalia—A Reception

The next town of importance is Visalia,[139] which is forty-seven miles from White River and about one hundred from Tejon, and the first town from Tejon. There are a few adobe houses, and the population is about five hundred. The place is situated in an oak grove, sometimes called the Four Creeks, which seldom have much water. There are a number of New Yorkers in the town, and I took a glass of lager, which made me feel quite at home. Though it was nearly midnight when we arrived, the news spread rapidly and we soon had a cordial greeting.

Before we left they gave us an anvil salute, which was quite new to me. The powder is placed in a hole in one anvil, and a train laid to the edge. A card is then placed

[137] Ormsby is confused at this point; actually, the Kings River is north of Visalia, and he mentions it later on.

[138] Bailey's spelling of Poso is "Posey." The stations between Poso Creek and Visalia were Mountain House, Fountain Spring, Tule River, and Packwood.

[139] In 1851, Nathaniel and Abner Vise settled at a place then known as Buena Vista, which gradually grew into a town. "Later, the name was changed to Visalia, a combination, it is said, of the names of Brother Vise and Sister Sally, his wife." (H. E. & E. G. Rensch and M. B. Hoover, *Historic Spots in California: Valley and Sierra Counties* [Stanford University, 1933], pp. 491-92.) Visalia became the county seat of Tulare County in 1853. See also K. E. Small, *History of Tulare County* (Chicago, 1926), I, 44-62.

over the hole, and another anvil on top of that. The
reports were quite as heavy as those of an eight-pounder.
This was the first evidence of any enthusiasm along the
route, since we left Fort Smith, and the rousing cheers
they gave us as we drove off at 11:50 on Friday, the 8th
of October, ought to be remembered in the history of the
town; so I here immortalize them. They were genuine
expressions of joy, for the mail of the 5th of September
from New York had but just reached them, while we
brought dates to the 16th. Our stations from Visalia were:
13 miles to Cross Creek, 13 to King's River,[140] 16 to Elk
Horn, 22 to Frezeneau [Fresno] City, and 19 to Firebaugh's Ferry on the San Joaquin. The road is over the
barren plain, with no wood except upon the banks of the
creeks, and no settlements except the stations.

A Large City—Fast Travelling

The soil is mostly alkali, and the taste of the water is
much tinctured with it. Frezeneau [Fresno] City is at the
head of a slough of the San Joaquin, and consists of one
finished house and one partly finished.[141] The proprietor
is boring an artesian well, for the purpose of obtaining
good water. From this point to the Tulare Lake the
course of a canal is marked by a furrow, which is, I believe, the only property of some anxious stockholders.

Firebaugh's Ferry[142] is the crossing place of the San

[140] Kings River was crossed at Whitmore's Ferry, which was established
by L. A. Whitmore, in 1854. See Rensch and Hoover, *op. cit.*, p. 151.

[141] This settlement, officially named Fresno City, and known also as Casa
Blanca, was eventually abandoned. It was located about one mile and a
half northwest of the present Tranquillity. See L. A. Winchell, *History of
Fresno County* (Fresno, 1933), p. 118.

[142] The ferry was established by Andrew D. Firebaugh (d. 1875) in
1854; he also constructed the Pacheco Pass road, which was completed in

Joaquin for the travel going to Fort Miller.[143] The mail route does not cross the river but runs along its southern banks to about the head of King's River,[144] when it takes a more westerly course and strikes through the coast range of mountains, at Pacheco Pass. We crossed the river, however, to get a good dinner and prepare for a pretty smart ride to and over the pass. The road along the river is excellent, passing through some fine land, though no settlements, except the station ranches, the owners of which own large herds of cattle, which we saw grazing on the plain or winding their quiet way to the river for water. There is no timber on the plain, but some on the banks of the river.

Firebaugh's Ferry is made a time table station, and we left there at 11:30 A.M. of Saturday, the 9th of October, and although that was something over six hours behind the time table, and the distance to San Francisco was only one hundred and sixty-three miles, we were still far in advance of the usual time, and had no doubt of reaching San Francisco in advance even of the time table time, which required the service to be performed in nearly one day less than the terms of the contract called for.

The road along the San Joaquin was one of the best I had seen, and our driver kept his team on the move,

1856. See Winchell, *op. cit.*, pp. 46, 164; P. E. Vandor, *History of Fresno County* (Los Angeles, 1919) [I], 425.

[143] Fort Miller was established May 26, 1851, and abandoned Oct. 1, 1864. See Hamersly, Pt. II, p. 145. It was located on the south bank of the San Joaquin River, near the present town of Friant. See Winchell, pp. 22-26.

[144] Ormsby is confused in names, as the Kings River is considerably south of the San Joaquin. Possibly the stage road turned west from the San Joaquin, near the point where the Fresno River joins it.

making the first twelve miles in one hour and twelve minutes, and the next twelve in one hour and ten minutes,[145] and the next eighteen miles to San Louis [Luis] ranche in one hour and a quarter, changing horses at each station and giving us some pretty fair specimens of the California stock. To run stage horses at such a rate of speed would, I judge, be considered rather dangerous work in the states, but here stock is cheaper, and if it does not last so long they buy more and keep the coaches moving along right smart.

The Pacheco Pass

From the time we leave Firebaugh's Ferry to the time of entering Pacheco Pass, a distance of forty miles, the Pacheco Peak is plainly visible. The San Louis [Luis] ranche is just at the entrance of the pass and is the only house within thirty miles. The building looks much like a country farmhouse in Connecticut, and the owner's hospitable table is always open to all who pass that way.[146] It is a great rendezvous for drovers going down into the valleys after cattle. The owner himself keeps about 1,400 head of fine cattle, which may be seen dotting the plain for miles around. He cultivates the ground but little, considering himself sufficiently well off to buy his supplies of those who do cultivate; while they in turn get high prices enough to keep themselves, doing as little work as possible. Few of these large ranches are owned exclusively by Americans, as most of them have been handed down from the old Spanish settlers. Much of the property,

---

145 The stations were Temple's ranch and Lone Willow.

146The ranch house was a frame structure built by Juan Pérez Pacheco, one of the original grantees of the Rancho San Luís Gonzaga. See Rensch and Hoover, pp. 189-90.

however, has come into the possession of Americans by means of intermarriage. The celebrated Chino ranche is thus now partly owned by two Americans, who, I believe, married two sisters, the descendants of the old Spanish owner.

As we entered the Pacheco Pass I had made up my mind to lie down in the wagon and take a nap, as night was fast approaching and I felt much fatigued. I heard the driver and agent, known throughout this section of the country as Tote Kinyon—the brother of the superintendent—remarking on the rough mountain pass which lay on our way; but, after the Guadalupe Pass, the Boston Mountain of the Ozark range, the Pacheco, and the New Pass, I had about concluded that I had seen all the mountain passes worth seeing on the route and that none could be more difficult or dangerous. But I was destined to be disappointed and to witness one of the finest views which the entire route affords.

The distance through the pass is twelve miles, and, instead of the cañon which I expected, I found the road to lead over hills piled on hills, which, though a little lower than their neighbors, were still at quite sufficient altitude. On every side we could look off down steep and craggy ravines, some of whose bottoms could not be discerned in the distance. Our road led immediately on the brink of many a precipice, over which a balky horse or a broken axle or an inexperienced driver might send us whirling in the air in a moment. There are also many abrupt curves in the road, winding around the sides of steep hills, on the edges of the ravines; many steep roads directly up and down the hills; and many rocks near the road, leaving just sufficient room for an experienced driver to take his team through without striking.

Fast Driving

Most drivers would have been content to drive slowly over this spot—a distance of twelve miles and every foot of it requiring the most skillful management of the team to prevent the certain destruction of all in the coach. But our Jehu was in a hurry with the "first States' mail" and he was bound to put us through in good time. I suggested to him that a bad man riding on this road was on the very brink of the bad place and likely to depart thence at almost any moment if anything should break. He said, "Yes, but they didn't expect anything to break," and whipped up his horses just as we started down a steep hill. I expected to see him put down the brakes with all his might but he merely rested his foot on them, saying, "It's best to keep the wheels rolling, or they'll slide"; so he did keep the wheels rolling, and the whole coach slid down the steepest hills at the rate of fifteen—yes, twenty— miles an hour, now turning an abrupt curve with a whip and crack and "round the corner, Sally," scattering the loose stones, just grazing the rocks, sending its rattling echoes far away among the hills and ravines, frightening the slow teamsters on the road and making them haul off out of the way, and nearly taking away the breath of all.

The driver seemed to enjoy the fun, and invited me up to ride with him on the box. I got up, taking off my hat and throwing a blanket over my head; I held on tight as we dashed along—up and down, around the curves, and in straight lines, all at the same railroad speed. The loosening of a nut, the breaking of a strap, the shying of

one of the four spirited horses, might—indeed would—
have sent us all to "kingdom come," without a chance for
saying prayers. But just as I made such a reflection, crack
went the whip and away we flew, at a rate which I know
would have made old John Butterfield, the president of
the mail company, and a very experienced stage man,
wish himself safely at home. For my part, I held on to
the seat and held my breath, hoping we might get through
safe. If I thought I was destined to be killed in a stage-
coach I most certainly should have considered my time
come.

We ran the twelve miles in an hour and five minutes,
and, considering the ups and downs, I thought it pretty
good travelling. The mountain is covered with stunted
oak trees, making it much resemble an orchard. On the
east side I noticed very few rocks, and none large. On
the west this was made up by huge rusty looking crags,
towering high in air, or with heavy boulders on their
sides or at their feet, as if just fallen. The road over the
mountain is excellent for the place and is much improved
by Mr. Firebaugh, who appears to be the enterprising
man of the region. He has a toll gate at the base of the
mountain, charging two dollars for the passage of a single
four horse team, which is cheerfully paid in consideration
of what he does to the road.

How the Californians Received the Mail

The next twenty miles, to Gilroy, we travelled in
two hours, and took supper. The scene here was much
like that at the other stopping places of any note along
the route since we left Franklin. The villagers gathered
around, asking all sorts of questions: "Have you got the

States mail?" "What's the news from the States?" "Is the cable working yet?" "Have you got any through passengers?" "Only the correspondent of the *Herald*." "Why, then, we shall hear all about it." "How did you like your trip, sir?" "Very well." "How did you manage to sleep?" "What, slept in the wagons?" "Did you ride day and night?" "Well, I declare, I should think you would be tired." "Have plenty to eat?" "What, beans and jerked beef?" "Glad to hear you say they'd have better soon." "Meet any Injuns?" "None at all, eh?" "Well, that's some comfort." "How long have you been?" "Left St. Louis on the 16th of September." "Well, that beats all stage ridin'." "Going to come through twice a week, eh?" "Well, that is good, now, ain't it?" "How's the line on the other end?" "Slow, eh?" "Of course, all the States people are slow." "Let 'em come out here and see a little life." "Here we do live—live fast, too."

A Croaker

I found, however, at Gilroy, one man who thought the mail wasn't such a tremendous thing, after all. He thought they hadn't made any good time yet, and he didn't think they were going to, very soon. He was the only croaker I saw the whole distance—the only man that was not glad to see the stage and to speak well of the enterprise. His name ought to be immortalized. I was glad to see Tote back him down on two bets as to the time when we would reach San Francisco.

Santa Clara County

We were now in Santa Clara County, one of the finest agricultural districts in the state, and Gilroy is one of its most flourishing towns, having over 600 inhabitants, a number of very fair houses, and several stores.[147] There is no claim on the town under the old Spanish grant. Thirty miles from Gilroy, passing through a valley of prosperous ranches, we came to San José, an old Spanish town, but now a small city of 3,000 inhabitants.[148] It is within fifty-three miles of San Francisco, to which point daily lines of stages run.

I should have mentioned, before, that the Overland Mail Company, through the energy of Mr. Kinyon, have been running a tri-weekly stage between San Francisco and Los Angeles, for nearly two months, using the Concord coach to San José and the canvass-covered thoroughfare wagons the rest of the distance.[149]

[147] "The first hamlet here was San Isidro [or Ysidro], named after the rancho of Ortega, into which family that early Scotch pioneer Gilroy, or Cameron, married. It gradually came to be known after this settler, but in time settlement shifted over round the inn established two miles off by J. Houck in 1850." (H. H. Bancroft, *History of California* [7 vols.; San Francisco, 1884-90], VI, 525.) John Cameron landed in Monterey in 1814, later changing his name to Juan Bautista María Gilroy. See M. B. Hoover, *Historic Spots in California: Counties of the Coast Range* (Stanford University, 1937), pp. 497-99.

[148] Bailey lists a station at Seventeen Mile House, thirteen miles from Gilroy on the road to San José.

San José, the first pueblo in California, was founded on Nov. 29, 1777. Its full name was El Pueblo de San José de Guadalupe. It was created the temporary capital of the state at the time the people adopted the constitution in November, 1849. By an act of the state legislature, the seat of government was removed in 1851. See O. O. Winther, *The Story of San Jose, 1777-1869* (California Historical Society "Special Publications," No. 11; San Francisco, 1935), pp. 3, 26; Bancroft, *op. cit.*, VI, 308-9, 321-25.

[149] According to the San Francisco *Bulletin* of Aug. 24, 1858, "the first stage of the Overland Mail Company over the southern route leaves the Plaza of this city tomorrow morning . . . and passengers will be taken through now as far as Los Angeles." The next day the paper reported the departure of the stage "this morning, at 6 o'clock, according to notice.

From San José the road leads, through San Mateo and San Francisco counties, to the city, having prosperous ranches ranged all along the line, with the flourishing little villages of Redwood and Santa Clara en route.[150] I was very sorry to be obliged to pass through this interesting part of the journey in the night—and a dark night at that; but the overland mail was on board and we made no stoppages other than to change horses at stations about ten

There were fourteen passengers, but none of them were booked to go through."

During the latter part of August and the early part of September, the San Francisco *Bulletin* carried the Overland Mail Company's advertisement which stated that stages left for Los Angeles on Monday, Wednesday, and Friday of each week, at 6 A.M. The time was changed to 10 A.M. on Sept. 3d, and to 1 A.M. on Sept. 16th. However, the newspaper of the 14th announced that the stage (the first one bound for St. Louis) would leave at 1 o'clock the next morning.

[150] Santa Clara, which was about three miles from San José, was not a stage station. The mission, Santa Clara de Asís, was founded on Jan. 18, 1777. A settlement sprang up around the mission in the late 1840's, and a townsite was surveyed in 1850. Santa Clara received its charter in 1862. See *History of Santa Clara County* (San Francisco, 1881), pp. 47, 539-45; H. S. Foote, *Pen Pictures from the Garden of the World; or, Santa Clara County* (Chicago, 1888), p. 205.

Bailey lists four stations between San José and San Francisco: Mountain View, Redwood City, San Mateo, and Clark's.

Mountain View, which Bailey records as being 11 miles from San José, was settled in the fifties. See *History of Santa Clara County*, pp. 262-63.

Redwood City is located on the former Rancho de las Pulgas. During the Spanish and Mexican periods it was known as Embarcadero. American settlement began in 1851; and in 1854 the town of Mezesville was laid out. The county seat of San Mateo County was moved there, from Belmont, in 1856. The name was officially changed to Redwood City when the town was incorporated in 1867. See P. W. Alexander and C. P. Hamm, *History of San Mateo County* (Burlingame, 1916), pp. 29-30; Hoover, *op. cit.*, pp. 441-43.

San Mateo is located partly on the former Rancho San Mateo and partly on Rancho de las Pulgas. By 1850 a few scattered settlers were in the district; but the town was not platted until 1863. See Alexander and Hamm, *op. cit.*, pp. 25-29; Hoover, pp. 438-40.

miles apart. It was just after sunrise that the city of San Francisco hove in sight over the hills, and never did the night traveller approach a distant light, or the lonely mariner descry a sail, with more joy than did I the city of San Francisco on the morning of Sunday, October 10. As we neared the city we met milkmen and pleasure seekers taking their morning rides, looking on with wonderment as we rattled along at a tearing pace.

In San Francisco—Delivering the Mails

Soon we struck the pavements, and, with a whip, crack, and bound, shot through the streets to our destination, to the great consternation of everything in the way and the no little surprise of everybody. Swiftly we whirled up one street and down another, and round the corners, until finally we drew up at the stage office in front of the Plaza, our driver giving a shrill blast of his horn and a flourish of triumph for the arrival of the first overland mail in San Francisco from St. Louis. But our work was not yet done. The mails must be delivered, and in a jiffy we were at the post office door, blowing the horn, howling and shouting for somebody to come and take the overland mail.

I thought nobody was ever going to come—the minutes seemed days—but the delay made it even time, and as the man took the mail bags from the coach, at half-past seven A.M. on Sunday, October 10, it was just twenty-three days, twenty-three hours and a half from the time that John Butterfield, the president of the company, took the bags as the cars moved from St. Louis at 8 A.M. on Thursday, 16th of September, 1858. And I had the satisfaction of knowing that the correspondent of the New York

Herald had kept his promise and gone through with the first mail—the sole passenger and the only one who had ever made the trip across the plains in less than fifty days.

Here ends my duty in describing the route overland from St. Louis to San Francisco, which I have discharged as well as information collected from the seat of the wagon would allow. The details might have been fuller had more time been allowed; but, such as they are, I think none others could show more conclusively that, whatever may be the difficulties in the way, the overland mail route may be considered as permanently established and its success placed beyond the possibility of a doubt.

To many Americans who travel for pleasure this route will be a favorite. Relieved from all danger from seasickness and the dull monotony of a sea voyage, they can travel by comfortable stages, stopping at such interesting points as they may choose for rest, and enjoying many opportunities for viewing the beautiful, the wonderful, and the sublime products of nature, which are well disposed the entire distance. The vast fertile lands, the romantic mountain passes, the large streams, and even the luxuriance of animal and vegetable life on the deserts, will attract the attention of the intelligent and give to the route a varied interest which a sea voyage does not and cannot possess. Already the applications at this end for passages can hardly be accommodated, and soon the company will have more passengers wishing to go than can be carried by long trains of wagons. The overland mail is, at any rate, a fixed fact.

Overland to San Francisco

Special Correspondence of the New York Herald
St. Louis, Sept. 16, 1858

Starting of the Great Overland Mail from St. Louis and Memphis. History of the Contract and Preparations for Its Fulfillment. The Competing Routes. The Arguments in Favor of the South Pass, the Albuquerque or Thirty-fifth Parallel, the Thirty-second Parallel, and the Extreme Southern Routes, and the Objections to Each. &c., &c., &c.

TODAY the first overland mail to San Francisco from St. Louis and Memphis, under the contract with the Overland Mail Company, started from this city, under the direction of Mr. John Butterfield, the president of the company. The contractors—Messrs. John Butterfield, Wm. B. Dinsmore, Wm. G. Fargo, J. V. P. Gardner, M. L. Kinyon, Alex. Holland, and Hamilton Spencer —are well known in your city as men of wealth, energy, and ability, and every confidence is expressed in their success.[151]

Thus is inaugurated, under the administration of Mr. Buchanan, a second great event of the age. The first

[151] For Fargo's biography see *Dict. Am. Biog.*, VI, 271-72. A. L. Stimson, *History of the Express Business* (New York, 1881), *passim*, contains some information about Fargo, Dinsmore, Holland (who was Butterfield's son-in-law), and Spencer. Nothing has been found concerning Gardner, of Utica, N.Y., or Kinyon, of Rome, N.Y. Ormsby, in a later article, says that Kinyon was the superintendent of the First Division, from San Francisco to Los Angeles.

linked two nations together;[152] the second cements a union
of the extremes of a nation separated heretofore by time
and distance, but now to be united by the facilities of
rapid communication; and both tend to bind more closely
those who before were united in the bonds of brother-
hood. The importance of an enterprise which is the first
practical step towards the Pacific railroad, can hardly be
overrated, and I think I may safely pronounce it another
great event of the age. If the overland mail succeeds, the
railroad and the telegraph will soon follow its course; the
settlements along the line will be built up with rapidity;
our vast possessions in New Mexico will be opened up
to us and to the world; and instead of a circuitous route
to our Pacific possessions, tedious in time of peace and extremely impracticable in time of war, we shall have an easy,
safe, and rapid route, where but a few years since nature
in her wildest aspect reigned supreme. It is in pursuance
of Mr. Buchanan's policy of developing the resources of
the country and studying its best interests, instead of truck-
ling to the political hobbies of the day, that these benefits
are to be gained. Under the supervision of his administration the great unexplored centre of our continent has
been thrown open to civilization. It has established a
route through northern Texas from San Antonio to San
Diego, a regular mail from St. Joseph to Salt Lake, from
Independence to Santa Fé,[153] and now the climax is capped

[152] Ormsby refers to the Atlantic cable which was completed the first
week in Aug., 1858, in the second year of the presidency (1857-61) of
James Buchanan.

[153] The route from San Antonio to San Diego is later described by
Ormsby as the "Jim Birch Route."

The contract for a weekly mail between St. Joseph and Salt Lake City,
begun May 1, 1858, supplanted an earlier one for service from Independence

by the successful commencing of this great enterprise. The theory that mountains separate nations, or that there lay between us and our California brethren an impassable obstacle erected by the hand of God, is thus scattered to the winds.

In view of the importance of this enterprise at this time, and the bearing which it has upon the future destinies of this country, I propose to give you a condensed account of the origin and history of the contract and the claims of the competing routes, so as to present in a condensed and clear light all the points of this question. In doing so, it will be necessary to refer to many places not familiar to the general reader; but I trust that the information imparted will be sufficient to repay the trouble of consulting what I confess is a rare article—a good map of the country west of the Mississippi. It may be, if all that is said against this route be true, that this is but the commencement of a trial for a wagon road to the Pacific, and it behooves every intelligent man to be thoroughly posted.

This is the largest contract for land mail service ever given, and—what is a curious coincidence—has to compete with a steam route which starts nearly at the same time. The six o'clock train today took a mail East to go by steamer to California, while the eight o'clock train took a mail West. Which will get there first?[154]

---

to Salt Lake City. See L. R. Hafen, *The Overland Mail, 1849-1869* (Cleveland, 1926), p. 109 n.

The first mail was transported from Independence, Mo., to Santa Fé, via Bent's Fort, in 1849; monthly coach service was inaugurated July 1, 1850, and improved to semimonthly trips in 1858. (*Ibid.*, pp. 70-73.)

[154] The overland mail from St. Louis arrived in San Francisco at 7:30 A.M., Oct. 10; the steamer "John L. Stephens," carrying the mail which had gone East by train, arrived from Panama at 5 P.M., Oct. 16.

The act of Congress under which this contract was made was passed near the close of the session, in March,[155] 1857, its father in the Senate being Mr. Gwin,[156] of California, and in the House, Mr. Phelps,[157] of Missouri. By the terms of the act [section 10] "the Postmaster General was authorized to contract for the conveyance of the entire letter mail from such point on the Mississippi River as the contractors might select, to San Francisco, in the state of California, for six years, at a cost not exceeding three hundred thousand dollars per annum for semi-monthly, four hundred and fifty thousand dollars for weekly, or six hundred thousand dollars for semi-weekly service, to be performed semi-monthly, weekly, or semi-weekly, at the option of the Postmaster General; [section 11] that the contract should require the service to be performed with good four horse coaches or spring wagons, suitable for the conveyance of passengers as well as the safety and security of the mails; [section 12] that the contractor should have the right of pre-emption to three hundred and twenty acres of any land not then disposed of or reserved, at each point necessary for a station, not to be nearer than ten miles from each other—provided that no mineral land should be thus pre-empted; [section 13] that the service should be performed within twenty-five days for each trip, and that, before entering into the contract, the Postmaster General should be satisfied of the ability and disposition of the parties, bona fide and in good

[155] Mar. 3. Ormsby's quotation of this act is substantially word for word. See *The Statutes at Large* (Boston, 1859), XI, 190; *App. to the Cong. Globe*, 35th Cong., 1st Sess., p. 25; Hafen, *op. cit.*, pp. 87-88.

[156] William McKendree Gwin (1805-85) served in the Senate from 1850 to 1861.

[157] John Smith Phelps (1814-86) served in the House from 1844 to 1863.

faith, to perform the said contract, and should require good and sufficient security for the performance of the same—the service to commence within twelve months after the signing of the contract."

You will perceive from this that the Postmaster General simply was "authorized," not required, leaving the matter entirely optional with the administration. Mr. Buchanan had too much the interest of the country at heart to allow this matter to pass by unnoticed. He paid personal and assiduous attention, with the Postmaster General, Gov. Brown,[158] to the manner of drawing the contract, and particularly to its awarding. You will perceive the perplexity of their position when Congress had left to them to decide the location of a continental route upon which themselves could not agree. The northern papers poured hot shot into their ears to compel the location at St. Louis, or at least further north; while the southern papers fired bombshells on behalf of the termini at New Orleans or Memphis, and the extreme southern route by Jim Birch's line, far below the thirtieth parallel, commencing at San Antonio, Texas, and extending, through the wildest portion of that state, west to El Paso. Columns upon columns were written to show the superiority of either or both termini. A most formidable array of statistics of population, length of railroads, amount of trade, and predominance of importance generally, were produced, and, amid the wildest excitement of all these interests, the bids were opened in June, 1857, and found to be as follows, from the present company:

John Butterfield, William B. Dinsmore, William G.

---

[158] Aaron Venable Brown (1795-1859), governor of Tennessee, 1845-47, was appointed Postmaster-General in 1857 and died in office.

Fargo, James V. P. Gardner, Marcus L. Kinyon, Hamilton Spencer, and Alexander Holland put in three bids for the semi-weekly mail, the common line of each being the thirty-fifth parallel, or Albuquerque, route, which I shall describe before I close. The bids for the semi-weekly mail were as follows: first, to run between St. Louis and San Francisco alone, semi-weekly, $585,000 per annum; second, to run between Memphis and San Francisco alone, semi-weekly, $595,000 per annum; and third, to run from both St. Louis and Memphis, converging at the best point (to be settled after a full examination), and proceeding thence on a common line to San Francisco, $600,000. This last was called the bifurcated route.

In addition to this, Messrs. Butterfield & Co. stipulated that they were willing to run over any variation of this route which the judgment of the Postmaster General might indicate as, from the result of experience, best likely to make the mail safe and expeditious. They were willing to alter any portion of this route which the Postmaster General might deem proper, either north or south, to avoid any obstructions that experience might prove to interfere with the safe and regular transmission of the mail. This idea of a bifurcated route (which, I believe, originated with Mr. John Butterfield, the president of the company) seemed to meet all the difficulty at once. It gave termini to both the North and the South, and no advantage to either. It met a difficulty which seemed to be insurmountable. But the Postmaster General and the Cabinet still held to the practicability of the El Paso route by the thirty-second parallel, and strengthened their opposition to the thirty-fifth parallel route by adopting the bifurcation, locating the converging point at Little Rock, and proceeding thence along the thirty-second parallel route.

Messrs. Butterfield & Co. fought hard for the thirty-fifth parallel, and were quite astonished to find that, though the act read "as the contractors may select," they had no voice at all in selecting the route upon which their money was to be expended. In vain did they protest that they could not run a line of stages to Little Rock. It was only after they had tried, and found it impossible, that the Postmaster General was willing to change the point of conveyance [convergence] to Fort Smith. Knowing the existence of this feeling of fear of the El Passo [Paso] route, an opposition member in the House introduced a proposition to have the route altered. But of course the contractors lent no countenance to an attack upon an administration whose employees they were, and it was unsuccessful owing to the vigorous opposition of Postmaster General Brown. The contract was signed on the 16th of September, 1857, just one year since, and provided that, whereas John Butterfield, William B. Dinsmore, William G. Fargo, James V. P. Gardner, Marcus L. Kinyon, Alexander Holland, and Hamilton Spencer have been accepted according to law as contractors for transporting the entire letter mail, agreeably to the provisions of the 11th, 12th, and 13th sections of an act of Congress, approved 3d March, 1857 (making appropriations for the service of the Post Office Department for the fiscal year ending 30th June, 1858), from the Mississippi River to San Francisco, California, as follows, viz: from St. Louis, Mo., and from Memphis, Tenn., converging at Little Rock, Ark., thence via Preston, Texas, or as near so as may be found advisable, to the best point of crossing the Rio

Grande above El Paso, and not far from Fort Fillmore; thence along the new road being opened and constructed, under the direction of the Secretary of the Interior,[159] to[159a] Fort Yuma, Cal.; thence through the best passes and along the best valleys for safe and expeditious staging to San Francisco, Cal., and back, twice a week, in good four horse post coaches or spring wagons, suitable for the conveyances of passengers as well as the safety and security of the mails, at six hundred thousand dollars a year, for and during the term of six years, commencing the sixteenth day of September, in the year one thousand eight hundred and fifty-eight, and ending with the fifteenth day of September, in the year one thousand eight hundred and sixty-four.[160]

Then followed provisions for the safe keeping of the mails, forfeitures in case of failure, the securing of the pre-emption rights for station lands, &c. A proviso was added, under which the route was changed, so as to converge at Fort Smith, by an order, "whenever the contractors and their securities should file in the Post Office Department a request, in writing, that they desired to make the junction of the two branches at Preston, instead of Little Rock, that the department would permit the same to be done by some route not further west than to Springfield, in Missouri, thence by Fayetteville, Van Buren, and Fort Smith, in the state of Arkansas, to the junction at or near the town of Preston, in Texas; but the

[159] Jacob Thompson (1810-85). Congress, in Feb., 1857, appropriated $200,000 for the construction of a wagon road from El Paso to Fort Yuma. See *Statutes at Large,* XI, 162.

[159a] The *Herald* reads, mistakenly, "or near to."

[160] See *App. to the Cong. Globe,* 35th Cong., 1st Sess., p. 25.

new line will be adopted on the express condition that the said contractors should not claim or demand from the department, or from Congress, any increased compensation for or on account of such change in the route from St. Louis, or of the point of junction of the two routes from Little Rock to Preston; and on the further express condition that, whilst the amount of lands to which the contractors may be entitled, under the act of Congress, may be estimated on either of said branches from Preston to St. Louis or Memphis, at their option, yet the said contractors shall take one-half of that amount on each of said branches, so that neither should have an advantage in the way of stations and settlement over the other. And in case the contractors in selecting and locating their lands should disregard this condition, or give other undue advantage to one of the branches over the other, the department reserved the power of discontinuing said new route from St. Louis to Preston, and to hold said contractors and their securities to the original route and terms expressed and set forth in the body of the contract."[161]

So far from neglecting to make preparations for carrying out this contract, the contractors have worked with almost superhuman energy to get the details in readiness. I understand they have bought horses and mules enough to have one for every two miles, and a wagon or coach for every thirty miles, of the route, while arrangements have been made at all the stations for changing the horses, feeding, &c., so that they can run straight through. During all their explorations and expeditions to complete the arrangements, they received the cordial co-operation of the

[161] Substantially word for word as given in *App. to the Cong. Globe*, 35th Cong., 1st Sess., p. 26.

Postmaster General and the War Department, and received the most gentlemanly attentions from the officers of the army at the various stations which they passed. I believe that, whatever others may think, the contractors are convinced that they will succeed in establishing this mail route regularly within a very short period, and you need not be surprised to learn that they have succeeded in establishing a daily mail to San Francisco within a year.

The adoption of this route was, as your readers are doubtless aware, attended with no ordinary difficulties, comprising, as they did, all the conflicting interests in the Pacific railroad. The schemes of speculating contractors and land jobbers, the jealousies of the various sections of the union, the clashing views of the railroad companies, and the machinations of politicians, all had to be met, conciliated, or overthrown; and, to the credit of the administration be it said, a steady, straightforward course has been pursued, in spite of the threats of the disappointed spoils seekers on the one hand, or the jeers and croakings of old fogy conservatives on the other.

It has been predicted that the contract for the route never would be given by Congress; that the contractors intended backing out of their agreement; that they never made any serious preparations to go on with the work at the appointed time; that the route was impracticable; that the mail would not run at the time specified, and that, if it did start, it never would go through in time, and probably not at all. Now, the contract was signed, sealed, and delivered; preparations have been going on vigorously for the last year; the route has been found practicable by parties sent out by the company to give them a private report; and the mails have started promptly and precisely at the appointed time and place. It only remains to be seen whether they will go through at all, and if so in the time specified. Your humble servant feels so confident that the men engaged in this work will not belie their reputation, and that the mail to California from St. Louis, overland, will reach its destination, that he risks the success of the enterprise, and leaving all that he holds dear behind will go through with the first mail bag, and give the readers of the *Herald* an impartial account of the trip, the difficulties—whether overcome or not, or likely to be— and all the information that can be gathered by rough experience as to the probable success or failure of the overland mail to San Francisco.

That there are difficulties, and no inconsiderable ones, to be met on this, as on all other routes, no one doubts. All accounts agree that the travelling is not quite as pleas- ant as in a Fourth Avenue car, or the fare as excellent as that of the Astor House, or the climate and temperature as agreeable as the shady side of Broadway in September; but, farther than this, I think I may say they do not agree. There were in all four prominent competing claims for

Overland Routes to California

First—Commencing with the most northern route, we have that from St. Louis and Independence, by the North Fork of the Platte, through the South Pass of the Rocky Mountains, via Forts Laramie and Bridger, to Salt Lake City, thence to the branch of the Oregon Trail, in latitude 42 deg., and thence almost direct to San Francisco.

Second—Taking the so called middle route, we have that by Springfield, Missouri, following the course of the

Canadian River direct to the Tejon Pass, via Albuquerque and the Mojave River, and thence through the Tulare and San Joaquin valleys via San José to San Francisco. This is generally known as the thirty-fifth parallel route.

Third—We have what is sometimes called the extreme southern route—though the term is somewhat a misnomer —from St. Louis, via Springfield, Fort Smith, Preston, and Fort Belknap, to Big Springs, on the thirty-second parallel, along which it passes to Fort Fillmore, Rio Grande, El Paso, whence it passes by Tucson and the valley of the Gila to Fort Yuma, by San Bernardina [Bernardino] to Tejon Pass, and by the valleys of the Tulare and San Joaquin to San Francisco. This is the route to be followed by the new Overland Mail Company, and is generally known as the thirty-second parallel route.

The fourth is the "Jim Birch's route," from San Antonio, Texas, through the valley of the Pecos to about the thirty-first parallel, thence via Fort Davis and the valley of the Rio Grande to El Paso and Fort Fillmore, along the thirty-second parallel route to Fort Yuma, and thence to San Diego.

These four routes had, all, their friends and zealous advocates. Those in favor of the first point triumphantly to the regular mail communication at present existing to Salt Lake City. The friends of the second brought the evidence of exploring parties of the government, and the favorable geographical location, being the nearest in a direct line from St. Louis to San Francisco. The friends of the third produced the testimony of government and private exploring parties, [and] the fact that part of the route had already been in use, under the "Jim Birch's" contract, from San Diego to San Antonio; while the friends of the fourth pointed to the fact that it had already been in successful operation for about six months. The eagerness of each of these interests—so vast as to include every section of the Union—may be explained by the consideration that the adoption of this new central route to San Francisco was regarded as the precursor of the Pacific railroad route. The northern states wanted it arranged so as to accommodate best their vast network of railroads. The Southerners wanted it so as to accommodate their trade and, it was alleged by some, in case of a dissolution of the union, to secure California. Here, of course, the politicians and speculators had a say, and the consequence was that, from the time the matter of awarding this contract for a great overland mail to San Francisco was agitated in Congress, to the time the contract was signed, there was a tremendous fluttering among all parties; and had it not been for the firmness of Mr. Buchanan's administration we doubtless should have been witnessing the fight still going on. Congress, after a most exciting fight over the subject, finally left the decision of the route to the Postmaster General, who, with the President and Cabinet, agreed upon the thirty-second parallel route, which is now going into operation. Just to give your readers an idea of the perplexity of the subject, and of the vast amount of conflicting testimony in relation to the different routes, I propose to give you in a condensed form the arguments which were advanced for each.

The South Pass Route via Utah

This route can hardly be said to have entered into competition with the others in the selection of the great overland mail route. Lying ten degrees north of El Paso and seven degrees north of Albuquerque, the temperature is almost universally conceded to be too cold to admit of the possibility of running stage coaches semi-weekly the year around,[162] as provided in the present contract. Gen. Burr, the Surveyor General of Utah,[163] found snow from twenty to forty feet deep during the middle of April, in the Rocky Mountain passes; and Col. Frémont found, in the mountain passes west of Utah, unmelted snow at the end of June.[164] Though a well watered and desirable route in summer, the terrible storms and snow drifts in winter, such as narrated by Col. Cooke, make its desolate regions entirely out of the question, when considering a feasible wagon route for the entire year.[165] The terrible sufferings of our army en route for Utah last winter[166] make this fact patent to every intelligent reader. Though the route was partially advocated by a certain ignorant journal in your city, which takes pains to imitate your

[162] Postmaster-General Brown, in his annual report dated December, 1857, said "recorded experience of many years" showed that it was impossible to procure "anything like regular and certain service" on this route. (*App. to the Cong. Globe*, 35th Cong., 1st Sess., p. 26.)

[163] David H. Burr (1803-75), appointed in 1855.

[164] John Charles Frémont (1813-90) recorded snow at his camp on the St. Vrain fork of the Elk Head River, on the west slope of the Rocky Mountains, about two degrees below South Pass, June 13, 1844. See his *Report of the Exploring Expedition to the Rocky Mountains in the Year 1842, and to Oregon and North California in the Years 1843-'44* (Washington, 1845), p. 281.

[165] Philip St. George Cooke (1809-95). A brief account of the hardships suffered by his command when marching into Utah in 1857 is given in H. H. Bancroft, *Works* (San Francisco, 1889), XXVI, 519-20 n., quoting from House *Ex. Doc.*, 35th Cong., 1st Sess., X, No. 71, pp. 96-99.

[166] Bancroft, *op. cit.*, pp. 517-23; Jesse A. Gove, *The Utah Expedition, 1857-1858. Letters of Capt. Jesse A. Gove . . . to Mrs. Gove, and Special Correspondence of the New York Herald*, ed. Otis G. Hammond (New Hampshire Historical Society "Collections," XII; Concord, N.H., 1928).

typographical appearance, it was never seriously thought of by any one at all posted on the subject. The recent success of the new mail arrangements have, however, rather enhanced its reputation as a summer route.

Jim Birch's Route from San Antonio to San Diego

This is the extreme southern route, and has already been run nearly a year.[167] It was highly appreciated by the Texans, southern states, and lower Californians, whom it most benefitted, and ran quite regularly once per month. It was for a long time pretty broadly hinted that Mr. Birch would get the present contract in spite of the demand of the North and West for a location which would be central for the Union. It was urged that Mr. Birch had fulfilled his contract faithfully and that, as it was to be in great part superseded by the new one, that he ought in compensation to be allowed to take the new one. The entire length of the route from San Antonio to San Diego is 1,410 miles, and from New Orleans to San Antonio about 586 miles, and has been described as a splendid natural highway, with an abundance of water, grass, and food for cattle, with but one desert of consequence to cross. An account of the first regular mail trip, which left San Antonio, Texas, on the 9th of August, 1857, and arrived

[167] James E. Birch was awarded the contract for this line in June, 1857, the service to be semimonthly. He was drowned on Sept. 11 of the same year, when the steamship "Central America" sank while en route from San Diego to New York.

Maj. I. C. Woods, Birch's general superintendent, carried on until the latter's widow sold out a few months later. For an account of the "Jim Birch route," see *The Texas Almanac for 1859* [Galveston, 1858], pp. 139-50; the account contains extracts from Woods's report to the Post Office Department.

at San Diego on the 31st, states that the entire distance was made in thirty-four travelling days, without relays.

The mail agent stated that, on the eighty mile desert between Tucson and the Gila, they found sufficient water in three or four places to supply hundreds of animals. No Indians were seen after they left El Paso, and but few before that point, though the second train was not so successful. The immigration at that time was quite large, and the trail has since been a favorite with all parties from the South and Southwest and from lower California. A strong effort was made to have this route adopted for the present contracts for weekly and semi-weekly mails, but the combined interests of the North and Northwest, having an eye to the establishment of a Pacific railroad route, as well as to accommodate their own vast trade, worked hard against it and succeeded in obtaining the new route which is now going into operation, as Mr. Birch's route obviously could be made of little or no benefit to the North or Northwest. It will be seen, therefore, that the great contest in the awarding of the present contract was between the thirty-fifth and the thirty-second parallel routes, both to start from St. Louis as a common centre; and, as the one had a host of warm friends and the other was finally adopted, I propose to give you a little fuller notice of them both than I have deemed necessary of the others.

The Albuquerque or Thirty-fifth Parallel Route

This route is from either St. Louis or Memphis to Albuquerque, on the upper Rio Grande near the thirty-fifth parallel, thence in an almost direct line west to the Mojave River and the Tejon Pass, and up the Tulare and

San Joaquin valleys to San Francisco. The geographical advantages claimed by its advocates are: that it is as nearly as possible in a direct line from San Francisco to St. Louis; that the first available passes through the Sierra Nevada and Sierra Madre, the farthest north which can be used during the whole year, are on this route; that the line is as nearly as possible an air line from San Francisco to New York; that the Canadian branch of the Mississippi on the east, and the Mojave River on the west, or, as Col. Davis noted, "the extension east and west, of inter-locking tributaries of the Mississippi, the Rio Grande, and the Colorado of the west,"[168] afford almost a right line of communication across the continent, desirable for both men and animals, in a journey of such length, for the supply of water and for the low passes unobstructed with snow; and the valleys of the Neosha [Neosho], Salt Fork, Red Fork, Arkansas, Canadian, Pecos, Galisteo, Rio Grande, Puerco, Rio Colorado, Chiquito, the Colo-rado, Mojave, and San Joaquin, which were comprised in the route, made it the best watered, the best wooded, and the best for the supply of food.

It was urged that Albuquerque is the principal town

[168] Jefferson Davis (1808-89), Secretary of War, 1853-57; see his "Report of the Secretary of War on the Several Pacific Railroad Explorations," I, 25. This report, with the reports of the engineers in charge of the various expeditions in 1853 and 1854, was issued as *Report of the Secretary of War, Communicating the Several Pacific Railroad Explorations. In Three Volumes* [hereinafter cited as *Pacific Railroad Explorations*] (33d Cong., 1st Sess., House *Ex. Doc.*, No. 129, Serial Nos. 736-39; Washington, 1855).

A revision of the *Pacific Railroad Explorations*, with additional material, was issued as *Reports of Explorations and Surveys . . . for a Railroad from the Mississippi River to the Pacific Ocean* [hereinafter cited as *Reports* (4to ed.)] (12 vols. in 13, 4to [Vols. I-X, 33d Cong., 2d Sess., House *Ex. Doc.*, No. 91; Vol. XI, 36th Cong., 2d Sess., Senate *Ex. Doc.*; Vol. XII (pts. 1-2), 36th Cong., 1st Sess., House *Ex. Doc.*, No. 56]; Washington, 1855-61). The citation, in this set, for p. 25 of Davis' "Report," is I, 20.

in New Mexico, which territory has from seventy to eighty thousand population and is best calculated to supply horses, cattle, and food necessary to sustain a mail route; that the passes are never obstructed with snow so as to prevent the use of the route the year round; and Capt. Whipple (United States Engineers) is quoted as authority that, in the highest passes of the mountains at this latitude, the deepest snow found was but eight inches deep, and the mercury was never down to zero, though the winter was unusually severe; that the only desert of consequence to be crossed was the space of thirty or forty miles west of the Colorado, said to be the only spot on the route where water could not be obtained at all seasons.[169]

The reports of Captain Ord,[170] Mr. Aubrey [Aubry] of Santa Fé,[171] and of Captain Whipple are all cited with particular reference to the practicability of this route. Indeed, it is said that an error was made in a hasty compilation of Captain Whipple's report to Secretary Davis, by

[169] Amiel Weeks Whipple (1816-63); see his preliminary "Report of Explorations for a Railway Route, near the Thirty-fifth Parallel of Latitude, from the Mississippi River to the Pacific," in *Pacific Railroad Explorations*, II, and extracts from the preliminary report, the revised report, and his daily journal, in *Reports* (4to ed.), III. For a description of Whipple's report see Wagner, *The Plains and the Rockies* (rev. by Camp), item 265.

[170] Edward Otho Cresap Ord (1818-83); his report of Dec. 30, 1849, was included in "Report of the Secretary of War, Communicating Information in Relation to the Geology and Topography of California" [Washington, 1850], in 31st Cong., 1st Sess., Senate *Ex. Doc.*, No. 47, Pt. I, pp. 121-22, and was re-issued in P. T. Tyson, *Geology and Industrial Resources of California* (Baltimore, 1851), pp. 121-22.

[171] François Xavier Aubry (1824-54); see "Aubry's Journey [July 10-Sept. 10, 1853] from California to New Mexico," in *The Western Journal, and Civilian*, XI, No. 2 (Nov., 1853), pp. 84-96. This journal and the one he kept of his trip, July 6-Aug. 16, 1854, are available in *Exploring Southwestern Trails, 1846-1854*, ed. R. P. Bieber and A. B. Bender ("Southwest Historical Series," VII; Glendale, Calif., 1938), pp. [351]-83.

which the El Paso and Fort Yuma route was made to appear two hundred and fifty miles shorter and eighteen millions of dollars cheaper than this route, when, on the contrary, this is one hundred and sixteen miles shorter and two hundred thousand dollars cheaper than the El Paso route. It was claimed that Secretary Davis made this error in his report to Congress, and that thereby the Albuquerque route was unjustly considered the most expensive and the longest, when, in reality, it was the cheapest and the shortest. The eulogium of this route by Capt. Whipple was unequivocal; and the fact that Secretary Davis reported to Congress in favor of the Texas route is attributed to the mistake above alluded to.

The official reports of the temperature of Fort Defiance, which is above the thirty-fifth parallel, make it appear that New York, Rochester, and even Washington, have all of them a much greater average depth of snow during the winter than Fort Defiance. All the sources of information seem to agree that this route is well provided with the means for supporting mail facilities, while its friends claim that it would well accommodate the body of the North, West, and South, taken as a whole.

In Captain Whipple's report he urges, with reference to its feasibility for a railway, that the first six hundred and fifty miles, from the eastern border of the Choctaw territory[172] to the river Pecos, passes, in the valley of the Canadian, a belt of country which is unrivalled in that longitude in its facilities for a railroad; that the fertile valleys would form the nucleus of new states, if thrown open to settlers and an outlet procured for the products of the soil; that the snow can never prove an obstruction

[172] The Choctaw territory is now part of Oklahoma.

to a railway; that the best general features are the inter-
locking tributaries of the Mississippi, the Rio Grande, and
the Colorado; that rainfalls are oftener in this latitude
than in the regions immediately north and south of it; and,
in short, that it passes through more cultivable areas, is
more abundant in supplies of water, and has a greater frequency of forest growth than any other route; while he
believes the heaviest grades that would be required would
be unequal to those now in use on the Baltimore and Ohio
Railroad.

Thus it was claimed for this route, that its geographical
position, and the results of scientific explorations, should
give it the preference, because San Francisco is but seventy
miles south of St. Louis, and this was the most direct route
through the most reliable passes—it afforded almost an air
line from Albuquerque to St. Louis—and was represented
to be the only one which insured an adequate supply of
water; that it was the route generally travelled to New
Mexico; that it was the shortest and most accessible from
St. Louis, and for the accommodation of the vast northern
and western trade, and network of railroads, and was best
calculated to build up settlements along its line. So ardent
were the admirers of this route in its favor, that one of
them used the following language, on the occasion of the
El Paso route receiving the endorsement of Postmaster
General and the administration:

Deserts, the Postmaster General will find, are beyond the government control, and impossibilities are not to be performed, even
though they are under contract and seal. Nor will the necessity
of concessions to the South, nor any such political considerations,
lower a mountain range or water arid plains, or make a wagon
road along the face of cliffs where a mule can scarcely keep his
feet. Politics are one thing, and geography is quite another.

Meetings were held at Van Buren, Fort Smith, and other places, to urge upon the government the adoption of this route. The report of Lieut. E. F. Beale[173] to Secretary Floyd[174] has also been cited at length in support of its claims—who went quite as far as either Aubrey [Aubry] or Capt. Whipple, and represented it to be the most beautiful country he ever beheld; three hundred miles shorter than any other route from the western frontier; the most level, well watered, and timbered, with plenty of grass, grain, and food, and the best climate that could be desired.

All this affirmative testimony would appear to be overwhelming at the first glance; but the question was by no means [so] one sided as to leave the Albuquerke [Albuquerque] route without a formidable competitor, with advocates who claimed to have seen some things which its friends claimed not to have seen. Capt. A. A. Humphreys,[175] of the Topographical Engineers, disputed that any mistake of the Secretary of War had created an erroneous impression as to the relative length or cost of the Albuquerque and El Paso routes. He attributed the difference between Capt. Whipple's first and second re-

[173] Edward Fitzgerald Beale (1822-93); see his report, "Wagon Road from Fort Defiance to the Colorado River" [Washington, 1858], in 35th Cong., 1st Sess., House Ex. Doc., No. 124 (repr. in M. H. Stacey, Uncle Sam's Camels, ed. L. B. Lesley [Cambridge, 1929], pp. [137]-281).

[174] John Buchanan Floyd (1806-63), appointed Secretary of War, Mar. 6, 1857, and resigned Dec. 29, 1860.

[175] Andrew Atkinson Humphreys (1810-83). See "An Examination by Direction of the Hon. Jefferson Davis, Secretary of War, of the Reports of Explorations for Railroad Routes from the Mississippi to the Pacific," in Reports (4to ed.), I. See also "Report upon the Progress of the Pacific Railroad Explorations and Surveys. November, 1855," in Reports (4to ed.), VII, "Conclusion," pp. [11]-18; "Report upon the Progress of the Pacific Railroad Explorations and Surveys. November, 1856," ibid., pp. [23]-34; and "Table Exhibiting the Comparative Lengths, Cost, etc., of the Different Routes, with Explanatory Remarks," ibid., pp. [35]-37.

ports to an attempt in the latter to demonstrate a possible reaction of distance between the Big Sandy and the Colorado rivers—a cut-off, the practicability of which had by no means been demonstrated. He claimed that the distance and cost of a Pacific railroad on the thirty-fifth parallel, from Fort Smith to San Francisco, would be 2,090 miles, at $106,000,000, and the distance and cost from Fort Smith to San Pedro by the same route was 1,820 miles, the estimated cost of road being $92,000,000, without reference to the cut-off from the Big Sandy to the Colorado. He estimates the distance and cost from the Mississippi to San Francisco, by the thirty-second parallel route, as certainly not more than that by Albuquerque or the thirty-fifth parallel; that the crossing of the great belt of the uncultivated country is better on the thirty-second than on the thirty-fifth parallel.

Just after the awarding of the contract for the thirty-second parallel route, and in answer to the croakings against the administration for the adoption of that route, an article appeared, said to have been published by authority, in which the following summary was given of the relative length of the thirty-fifth and thirty-second parallel routes:

Miles

Via Albuquerque, New York to San Francisco........3,297[176]
Via El Paso,   ”   ”   ”   ”   --------3,307

Thus, allowing a difference of length of but ten miles against the El Paso route, with reference to climate this authority makes the winter of the thirty-fifth parallel more

[176] This figure appears in the Postmaster-General's report in *App. to the Cong. Globe,* 35th Cong., 1st Sess., p. 28; however, the report gives the distance via El Paso as 3,351 miles, and says that 54 miles is "a difference too small to be a matter of grave objection."

severe than the statements of Capt. Whipple would indicate. It says that in Dec., 1855, the mercury at Fort
Defiance stood thirty-two degrees below zero at 6¼ A.M.,
and two hundred yards distant, in January, 1856, the
mercury ranged from four to eight degrees lower, and
there was not the slightest doubt that the mercury would
have been frozen had it been placed in a more exposed
position. The mercury was represented to have been below zero four mornings in December, 1855; six mornings
in January, 1856; three mornings in February; and below
on the mornings of the 1st and 2d of March. The winter
of 1855 was represented to have continued up to March;
the Rio Grande as frozen over; Indians as obliged to go
north [i.e., south]; and the depth of snow at the fort over
two feet at that time. This, the authority thinks, is enough
to settle the claim of the Albuquerque route adversely.
Captain Whipple was represented as having thrown too
much *coleur de rose* around his reports; and the records of
Fort Defiance, the reports of Captain Sitgreaves,[177] and
Captain Simpson,[178] and Dr. Letherman [Letterman],[179]
were all quoted to overbalance the testimony on the other
side, while the report of Captain Humphreys was exten-

[177] Lorenzo Sitgreaves (*ca.* 1811-88); see his *Report of an Expedition
down the Zuni and Colorado Rivers* (32d Cong., 2d Sess., Senate *Ex. Doc.*,
No. 59; Washington, 1853). For a description of this report see Wagner,
op. cit., item 230.

[178] James Hervey Simpson (1813-83); see his "Report from the Secretary
of War, Communicating . . . the Report and Map of the Route from Fort
Smith, Arkansas, to Santa Fé, New Mexico, Made by Lieutenant Simpson"
(31st Cong., 1st Sess., Senate *Ex. Doc.*, No. 12 [Washington, 1850]).

[179] Jonathan Letterman (1824-72), assistant surgeon at Fort Defiance.
The temperature readings which Ormsby quotes are to be found in "Extracts from the Correspondence of Jona. Letherman," in Smithsonian Institution, *Tenth Annual Report* (Washington, 1856), p. 287, and in *App. to
the Cong. Globe*, 35th Cong., 1st Sess., p. 26.

sively quoted from to show that, so far from being inferior to the Albuquerque route, the El Paso route was the best.

As a sort of clincher to all these authorities, Postmaster General Brown came out with an able letter, in February last, to the Post Office Committee of the House, in answer to an inquiry from the committee on the occasion of the effort on the part of Messrs. Butterfield & Co., the present contractors, to have their route located on the thirty-fifth parallel.[180] Mr. Brown called the attention of the committee to the fact that part of the new line had already been tested under the old Jim Birch contract; that it would be giving Messrs. Butterfield & Co. too much power to let them alter the route as they chose; that the contractors had already secured a modification of their contract in the permission to bifurcate at Fort Smith instead of Little Rock; that the selected line through El Paso was the best for the strengthening of new and desirable settlements; that he had fixed the route with as much consideration for the interests of every section of the country as possible; that the effort for the Albuquerque route was for the purpose of abolishing the Memphis branch altogether; that if that route was adopted it would have to have its terminus at Memphis; that physical obstacles made it necessary for the northern and western trade to go down to Memphis anyway, and they might as well go down the Mississippi, as, after they left St. Louis, the bifurcated route, which was adopted, converging at Fort Smith, was enough to satisfy all parties; and, finally, that the reports

[180] *Overland Mail Route to California. Letter of the Postmaster General to the Chairman of the Post Office Committee of the House of Representatives* (Washington, 1858).

of Captain Marcy,[181] Captain Pope,[182] and Mr. A. H. Campbell[183] all went to show that the department had done wisely in selecting the El Paso route in preference to Albuquerque for the great overland mail to San Francisco. But perhaps you will gather more negative testimony on this point in the résumé which I propose to give of the arguments, pro and con, in relation to the route now opening, and which has yet to be demonstrated to be deserving of the preference which it has received—the El Paso and Fort Yuma route.

The El Paso and Fort Yuma, or Thirty-second Parallel, Route

As arranged by the government, under the contract of Messrs. Butterfield & Co. now going into operation, this route commences at St. Louis and Memphis, converging at Fort Smith, on the western border of Arkansas, thence to Preston on the Red River, Fort Belknap on the Brazos, along the thirty-second parallel from Fort Chadbourne to Tucsan [Tucson], through the valley of the Gila, Fort Yuma, the Tejon Pass, and the valleys of Tulare and San Joaquin to San Francisco. In opposition to this route, it was urged that the road through the great Llano Estacado

181 Randolph Barnes Marcy (1812-87); his report on the route from Fort Smith to Santa Fé is included in *Reports of the Secretary of War, with Reconnaissances of Routes from San Antonio to El Paso* (31st Cong., 1st Sess., Senate *Ex. Doc.*, No. 64; Washington, 1850). For a description of the *Reports* see Wagner, item 184.

182 John Pope (1822-92); see his "Report of Exploration of a Route for the Pacific Railroad, near the Thirty-second Parallel of Latitude, from the Red River to the Rio Grande," in *Pacific Railroad Reports*, II, and in *Reports* (4to ed.), II.

183 Albert H. Campbell was with the Whipple exploring party on the 35th parallel, and with Parke on the exploration of the 32d parallel.

desert, the Hueco and Guadaloupe [Guadalupe] mountains, the desert plains of the Gila, and the Colorado
Desert, was impracticable for a four horse coach, being
afflicted with intolerable droughts, heat, and burning
sands, of interminable duration; that the grant of sections
of land every ten miles was of no use on these borders
of the torrid zone; the waterless plains of the Gads[d]en
Purchase,[184] and the burning sands of the desert and the
so-called Great Plains, had, respectively, grades of from
sixty-one to two hundred and forty feet per mile; that it
was deficient in the two elements for cheap construction
and working of a road—water and fuel. Especial attention
was directed to a table of the different distances to be
travelled in a torrid climate, over mountains, across plains,
and through burning sands, to obtain water, as follows:

	Miles
From the Rio Grande to the Rio Mimbres	71
From the Rio Mimbres to the Valley de Sanez [del Sauz]	72
From the Valley de Sanez [del Sauz] to San Pedro	89
From the San Pedro to Tuczon [Tucson]	53
From the Tuczon [Tucson] to Gila	79
Total	364

Even the Rio Mimbres, according to the report of
Lieut. Parke,[185] it was claimed, ought to be counted out,

184 For information concerning the Gadsden Purchase see P. N. Garber,
The Gadsden Treaty (Philadelphia, 1923).

185 John Grubb Parke (1827-1900); see his "Report of Explorations for
That Portion of a Railway Route, near the Thirty-second Parallel of Latitude, Lying between Dona Ana, on the Rio Grande, and Pimas Villages,
on the Gila," in *Pacific Railroad Reports*, III, and in *Reports* (4to ed.), VII,
under the title, "Report of Explorations for Railroad Routes from San

as it was but about six feet wide and one foot deep and often disappeared in the sands of the road. The reports of the same engineer on the same expedition were quoted for days in succession, and in derision it was asked, What a splendid country is this for staging—without water for fifty, sixty, seventy, eighty, or ninety miles, or a spear of grass or tree? Captain Pope was quoted as saying of the Llano Estacado, or Staked Plain—deriving its name[186] from a tradition that the Spaniards had staked a road on it from San Antonio, Texas, to Santa Fé—that it was without wood or water from the vicinity of the 30th to the 35th parallel, and was about one hundred and seventy-five miles across at its greatest width; that it was faced on its eastern side by an abrupt precipice over 500 feet high, and intersected on the south by a range of hills of white sand, destitute of vegetation, and seventy feet above the level of the plain, rendering it impossible of ascent for loaded wagons; that the shifting character of the drift sand would obliterate the trail and require constant labor to prevent the road from being buried; that it presents no inducements to cultivation under any circumstances—it was claimed that the cost of boring artesian wells would require $1,000,000; that stations could not be maintained even by a large expenditure of money; that it was trifling with the energies of man to ask him to run a four horse coach, either weekly or semi-weekly, over a route which could never be inhabited but by roving bands of bandits and Indians; that

Francisco Bay to Los Angeles . . . and from the Pimas Villages on the Gila to the Rio Grande."

[186] For variant versions of the derivation of the name see *Straight Texas*, ed. J. F. Dobie ("Publications of the Texas Folk-lore Society," XIII; Austin, 1937), pp. 17-21.

the bottom of the Gila, according to Major Emory,[187] consisted principally of dust and sand, overgrown with cottonwood; that the hills of the Gila Valley, with but few exceptions, were destitute of vegetation; that the deserts were whitened with the bones of men who had in vain endeavored to obtain water enough to support nature, and had miserably perished; that from the point where the Rio Brazos is crossed at Fort Belknap, to the Rio Peeds [Pecos], there was an entire dearth of water; that if the Texas route were adopted, across the sand plains of the Gadsden Purchase and over the great California desert, the enterprise would not only fail to commend itself to the business interests of the country, but it was exceedingly problematical whether the men and horses could survive the perils of the route; that it was a wonder how the four horse coaches were to be got over those long arid deserts on which the sunbeams poured so fervidly that one barrel of a double barrelled gun could not be fired without discharging the second barrel, from the heat; that, besides five hundred and sixty-nine miles of absolute desert, there were four hundred miles without constant water; that it would take years of time to make the route practicable at all; that the difference in favor of the Albuquerque route was four days' travel, or 391 miles; that, in brief, it was a barren, sandy, waterless, timberless, grassless route, without even the advantage of being of level and easy grade; that the circuitous route was adopted for the purpose of making it as much as possible within slave

[187] William Hemsley Emory (1811-87); see his *Notes of a Military Reconnaissance, from Fort Leavenworth, in Missouri, to San Diego, in California, Including Parts of the Arkansas, Del Norte, and Gila Rivers* (30th Cong., 1st Sess., Senate *Ex. Doc.*, No. 7; Washington, 1848). For a description of this report see Wagner, item 148.

territory, and to secure the building of a Pacific railway on the most southern route; that the enterprise was already regarded as a failure; that all persons at all acquainted with the country ridiculed the idea that the journey could be made in twenty-five days, as required by the contract; that a villainous band of land pirates and Gadsden Purchase, fact-suppressing Jefferson Davisites bargained for the overland mail through the sterile deserts of Arizona, whose burning sands and clouds would overwhelm and suffocate an army of dragoons; that the stipulations of the contract could not be fulfilled on account of natural obstructions.

Even after the contract was signed it was boldly alleged that the contractors never intended to work the route; that they merely went into the thing to make a stock speculation; and that it was utterly impossible to get the route in working order at the time specified. That ignorant journal which doubted your exclusive despatch with the news of the pacification of the Mormons, as also your exclusive despatch of the news of the complete success of the Atlantic telegraph cable, also said with reference to the contract and the contractors: "We believe it will be a total failure. The stipulations of the contract cannot be fulfilled because of natural obstructions which render its fulfillment impossible. There is reason to fear that the contractors bid off the contract without any idea of its responsibility, but with the general impression that it was the basis of a good speculation. There is no satisfactory evidence that the contractors expect to carry out their undertaking in good faith."

Now, I think your readers will admit that, when the contractors were met with all these objections, all this distrust, and these libellous charges, they must have had some spunk, to say the least, and that, if there is a tittle of truth in the many objections, their task in carrying out the contract will be herculean. But there were two sides to this question, as to that of the Albuquerque route, and I now propose to give you a few of the facts which were used in its advocacy and defence, leaving your readers to judge where the preponderance lays.

In favor of the El Paso route it was urged that the protection which would be necessarily accorded to the United States mail route would be but just to the citizens of the new territory of Arizona,[188] who were inadequately protected by the force then in that country; that, though the territory was more populous than either Kansas or Nebraska, it had no mail facilities; that it was equally exempt from the rigors of the winter of the northern route as from the terrible heat which had been attributed to it; that Mr. John R. Bartlett,[189] connected with the Mexican Boundary Commission, wrote an able paper, setting forth the advantages which from his personal experience he knew the route to possess—he stated that his party crossed the Llano Estacado desert without difficulty; that water was often found in several depressions; that wells might be easily sunk so as to procure water at all times; that the crossing of the Hueco range of mountains was without difficulty, or at least any but what was trifling; that there were fine watering places between the Guadalupe range and the Rio Grande, a distance of one hundred and ten miles; that the belt of country which is watered by the

[188] A petition for territorial status was first presented to Congress in 1856, but that status was not granted to Arizona until 1863.

[189] John Russell Bartlett (1805-86); see his *Personal Narrative of Explorations and Incidents in Texas, New Mexico, California . . . during the Years 1850, '51, '52, and '53* (2 vols.; New York, 1854).

Colorado, the upper Brazos, and the Red River, projects three hundred miles or more beyond the generally acknowledged limits of population; that the summit level at El Paso is but 3,800 to 4,000 feet, while at Albuquerque it is 7,000 feet; that, though slight snow has been known to fall at El Paso, the mercury would [not] sink to zero; that the district of country bordering on El Paso and Rio Grande is the wildest and richest portion of the bottom lands along that stream; that his surveying parties found water on the line of thirty-two degrees twenty-two minutes, between Dona Ana and Cooke's Spring, and in their various reconnaissances discovered water in many places not marked on the maps; he asserted that the valley of the Santa Cruz was the richest, and contained more land suitable for agricultural purposes than any between the Rio Grande and Pacific, within the belt between the thirty-first parallel and the Gila; and that the entire district from the Rio Grande to the Colorado, with its broad, open, gravelly plains, was well calculated for either a great wagon road or a railway. He represented the Pino [Pima] villages on the Gila as in a fine agricultural district, and the road to Fort Yuma as excellent. On the whole, he expressed the opinion that, poor as it was, the region was infinitely better than any yet discovered adapted for a route to California.

The famous letter of Postmaster General Brown, to which I alluded in my notice of the Albuquerque route, also presented some strong arguments in favor of the route adopted by the government. From a general view of the geography, meteorology, and physical character of the interior portions of the country, westward of the limits of the present population, Mr. Brown came to the con-

clusion that the march of empire must be in a southwestern course from the Mississippi River, and that the
conditions of climate were against the more northern
routes. He argued that the lower route was but ten miles
the longest, which, he thought, could not overbalance its
other advantages; that in climate, timber, and water, the
preponderance of evidence lay in favor of El Paso. He
quoted the testimony of Captain Pope, corroborated by
Captain Marcy, that between the parallels of 32 degrees
and 34 degrees "a broad belt of well watered and well
timbered country projects into the parched and treeless
waste of the plains," and approaches to within 300 miles
of the Rio Grande at El Paso. The uncultivated belt of
the desert, he said, was full 350 miles shorter on the thirty-
second parallel than on the thirty-fifth.

Of the countries beyond the Rio Grande, he quoted
concurrent testimony to show that the El Paso route
is well watered and timbered, has fine game and cattle,
and abounds in grain—quoting the explorations of Major
Emory, Captain Marcy, Captain Gray,[190] Commissioner
Bartlett, Captain Humphreys, Lieutenant Maury [Mow-
ry],[191] and other explorers, clinching the whole with the
report of Secretary Davis that "the El Paso route of the
thirty-second parallel is not only the shortest and least
costly route to the Pacific, but also the shortest and cheapest route to San Francisco." I can hardly better close this
résumé of the arguments in favor of the El Paso route,

[190] Andrew B. Gray, *Texas Western Railroad. Survey of Route, Its Cost
and Probable Revenue, in Connection with the Pacific Railway* (Cincinnati,
1855).

[191] Sylvester Mowry (1830-71); see his *Memoir of the Proposed Territory
of Arizona* (Washington, 1857). For a description of the *Memoir* see
Wagner, item 293.

than by appending the following resolutions, adopted at the Southern Commercial Convention held at Knoxville, Tennessee:

1. Resolved, That in view of the exposed and defenceless situation of our fellow citizens, residents of the Gadsden Purchase, and its peculiar and wonderful resources, it is the duty of the general government to extend over it that protection to which every American citizen is entitled; and that this convention fully endorses the justice of the memorial of the citizens of the Gadsden Purchase for a separate territorial organization, which is herewith submitted.

2. Resolved, That this convention looks with great interest to the successful establishment of the overland mail route to California via El Paso and Fort Yuma, and to the construction of the southern Pacific railroad; and, as the route selected by the Postmaster General as the great thoroughfare to the Pacific traverses the Gadsden Purchase throughout its entire length, the necessity for the proposed territorial organization becomes imperative for the protection of the territory, the travel and intercourse which must pass through it.

3. Resolved, That in view of the fact that a port on the Gulf of California is necessary for the supply of our Pacific possessions, Utah, New Mexico, California, and the Gadsden Purchase; and as the Mexican government, in the original treaty negotiated by our minister to Mexico, Col. James Gadsden, conceded a more southern boundary than the one adopted by the Senate of the United States, it is recommended to the government at Washington, in any future negotiation with Mexico, to acquire the boundary thus lost to us, and also a port on the Gulf of California, as a depot for the export and import of the great agricultural and mineral products of our newly acquired possessions.

4. Resolved, That the president of this convention do transmit to the President of the United States and the members of Congress from the states here represented, copies of these resolutions.

The following actual measurements of the distances by

the exploring party of the Overland Mail Company will
be of interest here:

	Miles
From St. Louis to Syracuse, Mo.	168
Syracuse to Springfield, Mo.	143
Springfield to Fort Smith, Ark.	175
Fort Smith to Colbert's Ferry, Red River	205
Colbert's Ferry (eighteen miles below Preston) to Fort Belknap	146½
Fort Belknap to Fort Chadbourne	136
Fort Chadbourne to Pecos River	165
Pecos River to Pope's Camp	66
Pope's Camp to Franklin (near El Paso)	172½
Franklin (through Arizona) to Fort Yuma	610½
Fort Yuma, on the Colorado, to San Francisco	664
Total distance from St. Louis, via El Paso, to San Francisco	2,651½

The distance from Memphis to Fort Smith, by the road
travelled for the present, is about 400 miles.

The letter mails leave St. Louis and Memphis at the
same hour of the same day, meet at Fort Smith and are
put into one bag, and proceed thence to San Francisco.
Passengers may with equal advantage leave either St. Louis
or Memphis for San Francisco, as travellers from those
cities reach Fort Smith at the same hour and travel to San
Francisco together.

These, in brief, are the arguments pro and con in
relation to the competing routes for the great overland
mail to California. The administration has selected the
last, and doubtless feels satisfied that the best interests of
the country are thereby benefitted; that the men to whom
the contract has been entrusted are those who in executing
their trust are merely carrying on a business in which

they have been for years engaged; that the prejudices of both sections of the country have been conciliated by the adoption of the bifurcated route from St. Louis and Memphis; and that it is so judiciously located, away from the extreme temperature of the north and the south, as to be certain of absolute success. The croakings of the disappointed spoil seekers and old fogies must, to some extent, be silenced by the fact that, notwithstanding all their abuse, the route is put in operation precisely at the appointed day and hour; whether the route is good and practicable I, as your representative, am to determine by my coming trip, and I hope that I shall not disagree with myself as much as the scientific gentlemen do with each other in giving a reputation to the route.

Although you have already published the time table of the company, I think it will be interesting to your readers to repeat it here:

Going to San Francisco

Leave	Days	Hour	Distance place to place	Time allowed	Average miles per hour
			Miles	Hrs.	
St. Louis, Mo., and Memphis, Tenn.	Mon. & Thur.	8:00 A.M.	—	—	—
P. R. R. terminus, Mo.	Mon. & Thur.	6:00 P.M.	160	10	16
Springfield, Mo.	Wed. & Sat.	7:45 A.M.	143	37¾	3.79
Fayetteville, Mo. [i.e., Ark.]	Thur. & Sun.	10:15 A.M.	100	26½	3.79
Fort Smith, Ark.	Fri. & Mon.	3:30 A.M.	65	17¼	3.79
Sherman, Texas	Sun. & Wed.	12:30 A.M.	205	45	4½
Fort Belknap, Texas	Mon. & Thur.	9:00 A.M.	146½	32½	4½
Fort Chadbourne, Texas	Tues. & Fri.	3:15 A.M.	136	30¼	4½

Pecos River (Em. Cross.)	Thur. & Sun.	3:45 A.M.	165	36½	4½
El Paso	Sat. & Tues.	11:00 A.M.	248½	55¼	4½
Soldier's Farewell	Sun. & Wed.	8:30 P.M.	150	33½	4½
Tucson, Arizona	Tues. & Fri.	1:30 P.M.	184½	31	4½
Gila River, Arizona	Wed. & Sat.	9:00 P.M.	141	31½	4½
Fort Yuma, Cal.	Fri. & Mon.	3:00 A.M.	135	30	4½
San Bernardino, Cal.	Sat. & Tues.	11:00 P.M.	200	44	4½
Fort Tejon (via Los Angeles)	Mon. & Thur.	7:30 A.M.	150	32½	4½
Visalia, do.	Tues. & Fri.	11:30 A.M.	127	28	4½
Firebaugh's Ferry, do.	Wed. & Sat.	5:30 A.M.	82	18	4½
Arrive					
San Francisco	Thur. & Sun.	8:30 A.M.	163	27	6

If the wagons keep up to the time table, the trip will be made inside of twenty-five days—that is, providing the roads are not unusually bad, and unforeseen accidents do not occur. As the mail leaves New York on the 20th by the steamer, there will be some competition. The steamer will be due in San Francisco on the 11th or 12th, and the overland mail on the 10th. Every nerve will be strained to keep up to time. The correspondent of the *Herald* will go through with the first mail bag, if it is a possible thing.

Appendix: Fort Smith to Memphis

FOREWORD

The Overland Mail Company experienced considerable difficulty in establishing satisfactory service on the Fort Smith-to-Memphis branch. The company had originally planned to transport the mail and passengers by water—down the Mississippi, and up the Arkansas River to Little Rock and Fort Smith. Shortly before the line began operation, however, it was found that boats were unable to go beyond Little Rock. As there was not time to equip and stock a stage line, Butterfield was forced to make a sublease to a stage company operating between Fort Smith and Des Arc on the White River, from which point the mail went overland to Memphis and passengers were transferred to boats.

The subcontractors failed to conform to schedule and trouble arose immediately. The second mail from St. Louis was delayed about thirty-seven hours at Fort Smith, waiting for the Memphis stage, and the San Francisco *Bulletin* reporter, six weeks later, waited nearly three days at the same point. The earlier eastbound stages carried many passengers booked through to Memphis, but, as it became known that transportation could not be relied upon at that end, passengers used the St. Louis route almost exclusively. Such neglect of their interests caused the people of Memphis to complain to the Postmaster-General.

Mr. Dundas, of the Post Office Department, wrote a strong letter to Butterfield on October 25, protesting against the subleasing of any part of the line and omitting Little Rock from the route, as entirely at variance with the stipulations of the contract. Further, he pointed out that the Postmaster-General would accept no inferior service between Fort Smith and Memphis. Butterfield answered that the company would assume complete superintendence of the line, and that every possible effort would be made to overcome the difficulties.

A small boat, the "Jennie Whipple," was purchased at St. Louis for $7,000. It steamed down the Mississippi on December 15, for service between Fort Smith and Little Rock; but, because of the low stage of the river, the attempt to carry the mail by water between these two points had to be abandoned. Butterfield then traveled over the line from Memphis, to observe what was necessary for its efficient operation. Before leaving the city he assured the people that they would soon have no further grounds for complaint. Equipment and stock were made available, and, on January 7, the mail arrived at Memphis on schedule.

The *Bulletin* reporter's account of his trip from Fort Smith to Memphis,[192] published in that newspaper and here reprinted, shows the condition of the route before Butterfield reorganized it.

[192] The complete account of the reporter's journey from San Francisco to Memphis was published in the following numbers of the *Bulletin:* Nov. 5, 6, 13, 17, 27; Dec. 20, 24, 28, 1858; and Jan. 4, 1859.

The sources of other information in the Appendix are articles in the San Francisco *Bulletin* of Jan. 10, Feb. 1 and 7, and Mar. 2, 1859; also a letter of the *Alta's* correspondent, J. M. Farwell, published in the *Weekly Alta California,* Dec. 25, 1858 (his journey from San Francisco to St. Louis is recorded in the following numbers of the *Weekly Alta California:* Nov. 13, 20, 27; Dec. 11, 18, 1858).

NOTES OF TRAVEL BY THE OVERLAND MAIL

From Fort Smith to Memphis
From Our Special Overland Correspondent

Memphis, December 6, 1858

Delays at Fort Smith and Des Arc

On my arrival at Fort Smith, on the 24th of last month, I then and there wrote concerning matters and things that I thought would be of interest to the readers of the *Bulletin*. After being detained there for want of conveyance for two days, until the morning of the 27th, I started in Reidsides [Reeside][193] & Co.'s tri-weekly coaches for the small town of Des Arc, situated on the White River, Arkansas, being 210 miles from Fort Smith. I reached Des Arc on the morning of the 29th, and was delayed there three days more, waiting for a steamer bound for Memphis, which I was fortunate enough to obtain on the evening of December 1st. I arrived at Memphis on the evening of the 4th.

Personal Adventure—Our Correspondent Drenched at Dardinelles [Dardanelle]

The only place of any slight importance, bearing the semblance of a village, was Dardanelles [Dardanelle],[194] which is nearly equidistant between Fort Smith and Des Arc—located on the Arkansas River. When we reached Dardanelles [Dardanelle], it was late at night, and raining in an old-fashioned way, worthy

[193] Lang, *First Overland Mail, Butterfield Trail*, p. 45 n.

[194] The county seat of Yell County. In 1820 a Cherokee Indian agency was located in this vicinity. The first permanent white settlement was made about 1842, and the town was laid out the following year. Dardanelle was incorporated Jan. 17, 1855. See *Centennial History*, ed. Herndon, I, 893.

of '49 memory. We were most unceremoniously turned out of
the coach by the driver and delivered into the charge of the
ferryman, who took the mail-bags on his shoulder, and, his lantern
in hand, told us to follow him to his boat at the ferry landing,
about one mile distant up the river. There was no remedy for
this unexpected tramp; so, placing our blankets on our backs,
and valise in hand, the passengers proceeded to accompany him,
through a torrent of rain, up the river bank and across the stream
in his small boat. It was well for the coachman that he could
not be found when we started on after the ferryman; he certainly
would have been roughly handled, as it was his duty to have
carried us to the ferry. We all got soaking wet by the time we
reached the coach on the opposite bank, and three of our party
were considerably used up, next day, from the effects of the
drenching.

Delay in Reaching Memphis

On arriving at Des Arc,[195] one of the passengers—that's myself
—waited for a Memphis boat, while three of them took a passing
steamer for New Orleans. The mail for Memphis was sent from
Des Arc for Memphis on horseback over the country—being a
distance of some 80 miles—while we was left to shift for ourselves
in the way of getting to Memphis. The company paid our fare
through. This was all right and according to agreement, but I
am certain that the department at Washington never contemplated that a delay of five days would take place owing to a want
of means of conveyance—being two days at Fort Smith and three
at Des Arc.[196]

The Route from Fort Smith to Des Arc

The road from Fort Smith to Des Arc passes over a very even
country, and through forests of oak. The soil looks cold, and

[195] The county seat of Prairie County. The first post office in the district
was established in 1831, but a town was not laid out until 1851. Des Arc
was incorporated Dec. 28, 1854. See *Centennial History*, ed. Herndon, I,
893.

[196] The *Bulletin* reporter was not aware that the Postmaster-General was
already in communication with Butterfield, concerning the poor service
between Fort Smith and Memphis.

much of the country is subject to overflow. We passed many farm-houses, and many fields were under cultivation—producing corn and cotton, but not, I should think, judging from appearances, in any great quantity. At many houses where we took our meals along the route, very little inquiry was made of us as to the nature and character of the route through, but there were always plenty of men and women to inquire about some Jones, Smith, or Thompson who had—many days, or rather years, ago—proceeded to California, and been absent, "*so, so* long—very long—ago, and never been heard of more." The fare on this portion of the road was of a very ordinary kind, but the sweetest dish that cheered our hearts was a roast opossum—though we saw nary coon—which I know is not the case with you San Franciscans, who, I suppose, see one daily in your walks along Montgomery Street.

The White River

It is about 300 miles from Memphis to Des Arc by water, and about 80 or 90 by land. White River is a very beautiful stream, free from snags, and resembles in size and appearance the Sacramento. I enclose a card of landings and distances. <This has not come to hand. It was probably overlooked in sealing our correspondent's package.> The stream abounds in trout, perch, and cat-fish, and the passengers amused themselves in shooting geese and ducks from the steamer's deck. It has been raining every day since we left Des Arc—sometimes nearly all day, and then a slight sprinkle the next. The steamer "Return," on which I came, brought any quantity of game—such as deer, ducks, geese, turkeys, prairie hens, wild pigeons, and partridges, all of which appeared in fine condition.

Entering the Mississippi—Thoughts Suggested by It

It was near night when we entered the Mississippi River. Its muddy waters rolled quietly along as though ten thousand skeletons, the victims of steamboat accidents, lay not beneath its surface. No one, after a long absence from the shores of the Mississippi, can contemplate its mighty stream without feelings of awe, amounting almost to trepidation. On each side stand the tall, slender cottonwood trees and the buoyant willows, high up on the trunks of which are the watermarks of the late overflow. Steamers of giant proportions and costly decoration float on its muddy tide, while below the surface of its waters the alligator rattles in his toils the bones of the dead. It may be said with truth that this river has cost more lives than ever it has made fortunes. We passed the wreck of the steamer "Pennsylvania," on our way up, lying between this city and the mouth of White River—in the blowing up of which 250 lives were lost. I think it would take many days to make two hundred and fifty fortunes. When we take into consideration the number of steamboats constantly running up and down the Mississippi, the wonder is, not that so many lives are lost, but that more human beings are not destroyed through accident.

Nearly nine years ago, I left the mouth of this famous river, on a journey round the Horn for California, and after so long an interval of time I have returned to its banks, a wiser, I hope, if not a richer man. One knows not whether the flight of Time is the same through all space and over all lands and seas, but it seems to me that his minutes to me, since I left California, have grown into hours, and that he lags in his speed and moves not with such velocity as he was wont in the bracing air of the Pacific.

Description of Memphis

Memphis is, as most of the readers of the *Bulletin* are doubtless aware, located on the east bank of the Mississippi River, 900 miles from the Gulf of Mexico, by the course of the river. Its population is about 30,000, with a daily floating population of some 2,500. The city is about two miles long and one mile wide, with a suburban belt quite closely settled. . . . [197]

[197] Omitted matter relates principally to the city.

Index

173

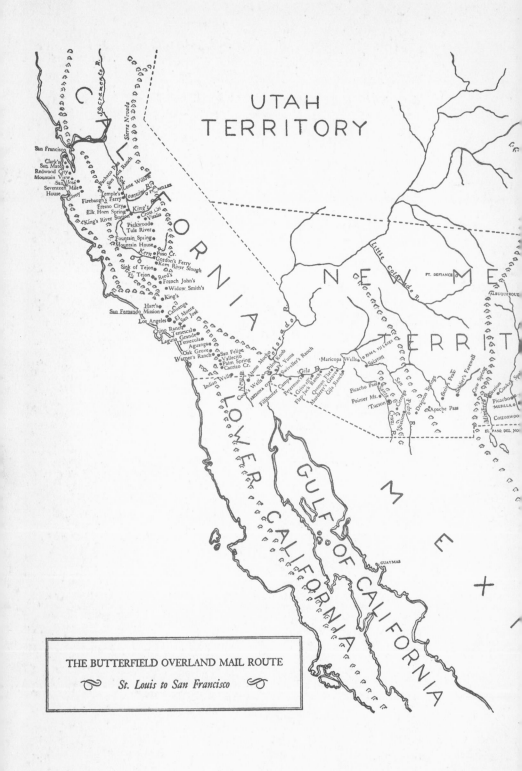

THE BUTTERFIELD OVERLAND MAIL ROUTE

St. Louis to San Francisco